JOY IN THE MORNING

Dyron Daughrity

Keledei
PUBLICATIONS

An Imprint of Sulis International Press
Los Angeles | Dallas | London

JOY IN THE MORNING

Copyright ©2025 by Dyron Daughrity. All rights reserved.

All rights reserved. No part of this book may be reproduced in any form or by any means without the prior written consent of the Publisher, excepting brief quotes used in reviews.

ISBN (print): 978-1-958139-59-2
ISBN (eBook): 978-1-958139-60-8

Published by Keledei Publications
An Imprint of Sulis International
Los Angeles | Dallas | London

www.sulisinternational.com

Contents

1. Joy in the Morning 1
2. Tapping into the True Source of Joy 11
3. Throw Away the List of Wrongs 23
4. Suffering Leads to Joy 33
5. Don't Become Bitter 43
6. Choose Your Companions Wisely 55
7. Be a Generous Person 65
8. Don't Panic. Turn to God 77
9. Joy is Medicine for the Soul 89
10. Joy is Found in Community 99
11. The Joy of Heaven 109
12. Have an Attitude of Gratitude 121

1. Joy in the Morning

One day, a friend of mine stopped me at Pepperdine to ask how I was doing. I told him I was doing fine, and that the real question is how he is doing. This friend, you see, has an incurable form of lymphoma. He is in remission, but this is the second time he has been in remission since he was first diagnosed in late 2022. He took an experimental treatment that worked, but he is not cancer free. In fact, he has been told that the cancer will come back; that it's only a matter of time. His doctor recently said these words to him: "This kind of cancer always comes back– 'intermission' is a more accurate term than 'remission.'"

Despite these circumstances, my friend has true joy. Here's what he wrote in his latest email:

Before cancer, my career and family life ranked as pretty good on the human scale. I was content. My health was robust. Life was not without serious challenges, sorrows, and sinful failings, but my wife and I were happy ... I knew that there was no part of my existence that I could insulate from God's loving plans. The best part of me did not want to block off anything from God's grace. Nevertheless, part of me simply wanted to reign, to pursue at least some of my projects as if they did not concern God, or as if He were uninterested in them. Even when my actions ... were good ... in themselves, my desire to be my own master often closed me to God's grace, and consequently darkened my soul.

In this book, I am focusing intensely on the concept of joy. Joy may oftentimes seem like a superficial emotion, like a synonym for "happy." But the joy of the Lord is something else. It is rooted in a deeper place within us. You can be struggling with cancer and still have the joy of the Lord inside you. You can also, ironically, appear happy on the outside but have a "darkened soul." The advertisers of the world teach us that the new object of our desires—a car, a phone, a certain salary, a particular job—will make us happy. But time and again, we are reminded that "stuff" will never give us deep joy.

As human beings, we chase things, deceiving ourselves to believe we'll have true satisfaction and joy once we get it. But when we get that thing, that person, that salary, we are bluntly reminded that people and things don't provide inner joy. Why? Because inner joy comes from someplace else. Inner joy comes only from the Lord.

If we try to attain joy through other things, we are likely to end up in a dark place. My friend spoke of having a darkened soul—feeling darkened on the inside. Experiencing spiritual and mental darkness. My hope and prayer is that this book will convince you to take steps in the right direction in your pursuit of the good life, to free your soul from darkness. Hopefully, this will point you towards the true source of joy. In some chapters, I will talk little about joy, and more about the underlying issues that produce the outcome of joy. But there is a lot of work that must be done if we are going to attain our desired outcome—of having great joy in life.

As with any substantial goal, there is a lot of spade work that goes on before you get the outcome you want. If you want to marry an amazing person, then there's a lot of work to be done—because you're not going to attract an amazing person if you are not an amazing person. Instead of chasing amazing people, you must work on yourself. You must change your priorities. You have to become the best version of yourself. You'll have to put in hours and hours of work that entails tremendous discipline. You'll have to be open to changing yourself from within. Then, one day, you'll look in the mirror and realize how far you've come. Before you know it, you'll find some amazing people in your life. Why? Because they want to be around amazing people, and you have become an amazing person. But it took time. It took work.

That's what this book is all about.

Why did I title this book "Joy in the Morning?" It's because of this: if you can begin a day with joy, then you will start off strong. The goal is to have joy when you wake up. You don't have to wait until 5pm to have joy. You can have it in the morning.

There is a deeper meaning to this title as well. You may be in a season of struggle. You may just now be emerging from a "dark night of the soul." Or perhaps you are walking through "the valley of the shadow of death," so to speak. But no matter where you are, "There will be joy in the morning."

Psalm 30:5 (KJV) says this: "Weeping may endure for a night, but joy cometh in the morning."

Yes, there will be joy– in the morning. As a child of God, you must cling on to that hope—that joy will come. It will eventually come. In that same Psalm (30:2-3, 11), David says this (NIV):

> Lord my God, I called to you for help,
>   and you healed me.
>   You, Lord, brought me up from the realm of
> the dead;
>   you spared me from going down to the pit.
>   You turned my wailing into dancing;
>   you removed my sackcloth and clothed me
> with joy.

You may be struggling now or have struggled in the past. But hang in there. Don't give up. There is a morning that is coming. And there will be joy in the morning.

We are not talking about happiness in this book. The two words are often used interchangeably, but they're not the same thing. Happiness tends to be about pleasure. That movie made me happy. I got a raise today, and it makes me happy. I am happy that my team won the game last night.

Joy, however, is a state of mind that persists even when present circumstances are not exactly how we want them. I can have joy even if three things went wrong this morning—I awoke to realize my washing machine is broken, a car cut me off in traffic on the way to work, and nobody talked to me as I entered the church building and took my seat. Normally, a trifecta of disappointing things will put people into a pessimistic, dour, ugly mood. But joy can vanquish all of that. A joyful heart can see the bigger picture. A joyful outlook says, "That's right … things aren't going so well today …. But I'm okay. I am not immune from bad luck. Just because I'm a Christian doesn't mean I'm protected from bad days. But, hey, I still have many things to be thankful for."

Joy changes your perspective. You'll begin to say things like this:

I may be unsettled by a broken washing machine, but there are more important things in the world. This is not a huge thing. Last time it broke, I got it fixed. Living for Jesus is so much more important. And I don't want to enter a dark place because of something—like a washing machine—that is completely outside of my control. This is one, little thing that will soon be fixed. And I'm not going to let it get to me. God has great things in store for me today, and I'm not going to let something so small destroy my peace of mind or rob me of the joy I can share with others today.

Joy is deep. It requires discipline to get to a place of joy. It requires work. It requires time in the Lord's presence, so you know who you are, so you won't let the opinions of others destroy you. Joy keeps you thinking rationally, and it helps you to maintain a steady outlook on life, rather than going UP DOWN, UP DOWN. Joy in your heart will calm you down from the inside. The fact that you got cut off in traffic doesn't matter. You'll remember there are things in life that just aren't important in the grand scheme.

Recently, I had a friend call me. He was in need. He was suffering because a person at work was really annoying him. Their offices are very close to each other, so my friend was unable to escape seeing this person every day. My friend seethed for over two months.

I took my friend for a walk. We talked late into the night. I told him, "Look, this fellow is destroying you! He is turning you into something you don't want to become! You are walking around every day, upset at everything, all because this guy bothers you. Brother, my advice for you is to cut this guy out of your mind. Yes, you'll see him in the hallway, but you've got to take your mind off him. You're thinking about the wrong things!"

This book is going to remind us repeatedly that what we think about is so crucial. If you think about good things, you will be more likely to find yourself in a bright place. If you go down rabbit holes of bitterness, vengeance, and how badly you've been hurt, then unfortunately your mind will follow. My hope is that these words will direct you to God's Word because only there will you find the true source of joy.

Listen to these words from Paul (Ephesians 4:17-24):

> So I tell you this, and insist on it in the Lord,
> that you must no longer live as the Gentiles do,
> in the futility of their thinking. They are dark-

ened in their understanding and separated from the life of God because of the ignorance that is in them due to the hardening of their hearts. Having lost all sensitivity, they have given themselves over to sensuality so as to indulge in every kind of impurity, and they are full of greed.

That, however, is not the way of life you learned when you heard about Christ and were taught in him in accordance with the truth that is in Jesus. You were taught, with regard to your former way of life, to put off your old self, which is being corrupted by its deceitful desires; to be made new in the attitude of your minds; and to put on the new self, created to be like God in true righteousness and holiness.

My prayer is that this book, rooted in scripture, will help us all leave behind our "old self," and get in better touch with our "new self"—the self that is anchored in Christ, and infused with the Holy Spirit. Sensuality, greed, hardening of the heart, separation from God, insensitivity... as the apostle Paul says, these things characterize the "old self." This is the path to self-destruction. Indeed, this is the path to hell. But the "new self" involves a completely different mindset. Here's what the apostle Paul says is going on in the head of someone who lives according to the "new self" (Philippians 4:8):

> ... Whatever is true, whatever is noble, whatever is right, whatever is pure, whatever is lovely, whatever is admirable—if anything is excellent or praiseworthy—think about such things.

Instead of thinking about everything that is wrong ... think about things that are right in your life. You are what you think. Instead of thinking impure thoughts, think pure thoughts. Instead of thinking about how to criticize someone, think about how you admire them. Instead of thinking about mistakes people have made, think about things are that are excellent or praiseworthy in those same people. There is one thing you have control over in this world. You get to choose what you think about. And you can change the way you think. You can alter your mind and direct it towards good thoughts.

It's so sad that people—ourselves included—easily get into bad habits of thinking. Really ugly habits. People get consumed by fear. They are afraid they are going to fail. Afraid they won't be accepted. Afraid of a catastrophe that is about as unlikely as a snowstorm in Barstow. We die a thousand deaths in our minds. People focus on the trials of life, rather than the blessings of life. They focus on everyone who has wronged them. They get so bitter. Some people have days where about 92% of it went well, but they want to focus on that 8% that didn't go well.

Some folks begin to really pity themselves. Instead of counting their blessings, they get obsessed with how they were slighted at work. Or how their boss doesn't recognize them.

My prayer is that this book will help us all to think better. If our boss doesn't recognize us, then we've got to learn how to think differently about the situation. If we keep obsessing on the boss who isn't quite what we want, then we're going to live frustrated, and we'll cheat our children, our friends, and our spouse out of our best self. We'll become an inferior version of ourselves. If we keep thinking like this, then eventually our soul could become dark. That's a place we don't want to go.

As a free gift, I'm going to give you the secret to a better countenance, better skin, and better bones. That's a big promise! So ... do you want to look better, fresher, even younger than you do? Here's the recipe, found in Proverbs 15:13, and 17:22,

> A happy heart makes the face cheerful,
>   but heartache crushes the spirit.
> A cheerful heart is good medicine,
>   but a crushed spirit dries up the bones.

In conclusion, this book is going to help you get your joy back. If you pour yourself into scripture and into the guidance this text provides, then you are going to have joy in your heart, no matter what you're dealing with in your life.

Let us get our joy back. Even if you are dealing with something heavy, like my friend who is dealing with lymphoma, or the beloved preacher at Hilltop whose wife is fighting brain cancer. Just because you are dealing with major challenges does not mean you should walk around sad, fearful, and in despair.

Homework

To close this chapter, I want to ask you to do something. I want to ask you to do a self-evaluation. What is keeping you from having true and pure joy? I want you to physically write down what is robbing you of joy on a piece of paper, or on your phone, and talk to a loved one or church leader about it.

You can get your joy back. Let's have some fun on this journey together.

2. Tapping into the True Source of Joy

In this second chapter on the concept of joy we are diving into ways to "tap into the true source of joy." I asked you in the last chapter to document the circumstances in your life preventing you from having joy—your "joy-busters." When I asked my congregation "What is robbing you of joy?" numerous people reached out to me, mainly by text. A few people emailed me, and one person gave me a piece of paper. I wanted to break these down so we can all get a sense of what people are dealing with. Here's what people's "joy-busters" are:

- A messy house
- Financial fear
- Addiction issues
- Fear
- Guilt and regret
- Worrying about my children
- Anxiety and worry

- Not enough quality time with the people I love.
- People who lie.
- Politics
- Co-workers.
- Negative people.
- Problems in the workplace.
- Frustrations with people.
- Stress
- Needing to find a permanent place for my mentally disabled adult child.
- My long-term medical condition.
- People's attitudes towards me.
- Thinking too much about what I don't have.
- Hopelessness.
- My own failings.
- The news steals my joy!
- My phone.
- Racism.
- My drinking problem.

As I said at the end of the last chapter, you CAN get your joy back. We're on a journey together. I believe, strongly, that we can each deal with these problems.

And we can overcome them. Eventually, with some work, we can get our joy back.

The topic of this chapter is "Tapping into the True Source of Joy."

And what is the "true source" of joy? It is our relationship with Jesus Christ. That's where true, inner joy is found in its purest form. When we connect to Jesus Christ, when we walk closely with Him, then we have joy. When we distance ourselves from Jesus, our hearts become darkened. We become sad. Anxious. Depressed. We want to give up. Or we resort to sinful things more easily. And one thing we all know is this: "Sin steals our joy."

Jesus tells us something very important in John 10:9-10. Read this verse:

> I am the gate; whoever enters through me will
> be saved. They will come in and go out, and
> find pasture. The thief comes only to steal and
> kill and destroy; I have come that they may
> have life, and have it to the full.

Who is "the thief?" It is the devil! When we walk away from Christ, we walk into the arms of the devil. He promises us pleasure, but when we listen to him, we realize we have been lied to. We end up feeling used. The only way to avoid this darkness is by staying close to Jesus. By walking into His gate each morning, whenever we wake up, we experience "Joy" first thing in the morning. Open each day with a prayer, and you'll find yourself on the right path.

Sin steals joy. These three words are crucial for us. *Sin steals joy.* You may get a quick hit of pleasure from sin, but joy is diminished.

The problem is that sin feels good in the moment: gossip, lust, bursts of anger, "venting" to someone about someone, hating someone... all of this may feel good for a bit of time, but it backfires. The apostle Paul says this in Romans 6:23,

> The wages of sin is death, but the gift of God is eternal life in Christ Jesus, our Lord.

Sin has a price. The price is death. Death to your joy. Death to your relationships. Death to your confidence. And, eventually, if it consumes you, potentially death to your soul.

Hear the gospel: *Jesus Christ is the true source of joy.* Hear these words from our Lord (John 16:20-24):

> Very truly I tell you, you will weep and mourn while the world rejoices. You will grieve, but your grief will turn to joy. A woman giving birth to a child has pain because her time has come; but when her baby is born, she forgets the anguish because of her joy that a child is born into the world. So with you: Now is your time of grief, but I will see you again and you will rejoice, and no one will take away your joy. In that day, you will no longer ask me any-thing. Very truly I tell you, my Father will give you whatever you ask in my name. Until now you have not asked for anything in my name.

> Ask and you will receive, and your joy will be complete.

Don't give up hope. As our Lord Jesus tells us, "your grief will turn to joy." There will be joy in the morning. Joy is coming. You can get your joy back.

Joy is part of being a Christian. And when you are "in Christ," you will notice the joy. In Galatians chapter 5, the apostle Paul tells us that "joy" is part of the fruit of the Spirit. In John 15:11, Jesus says this:

> "I have told you this so that my joy may be in you and that your joy may be complete."

The Lord wants us to experience joy. Yes, there is a time for sorrow. There is a time to mourn. But part of living the Christian life is having a foundation of joy. The Lord wants us to have joy because it is strength for us. This is said in Nehemiah 8:10b, "Do not grieve, for the joy of the Lord is your strength."

Several heartening passages of scripture have been brought to your attention in this chapter thus far, but right now, I want to introduce you to the most important passage, I believe, of this chapter. It is found in John 15:1-11,

> I am the true vine, and my Father is the gardener. He cuts off every branch in me that bears no fruit, while every branch that does bear fruit he prunes so that it will be even more fruitful. You are already clean because of the word I have spoken to you. Remain in me, as I also remain

> in you. No branch can bear fruit by itself; it must remain in the vine. Neither can you bear fruit unless you remain in me.
>
> I am the vine; you are the branches. If you remain in me and I in you, you will bear much fruit; apart from me you can do nothing. If you do not remain in me, you are like a branch that is thrown away and withers; such branches are picked up, thrown into the fire and burned. If you remain in me and my words remain in you, ask whatever you wish, and it will be done for you. This is to my Father's glory, that you bear much fruit, showing yourselves to be my disciples.
>
> As the Father has loved me, so have I loved you. Now remain in my love. If you keep my commands, you will remain in my love, just as I have kept my Father's commands and remain in his love. I have told you this so that my joy may be in you and that your joy may be complete.

Again, why did Jesus share this with us? It is so that we would have joy. *HIS* joy. And "his" joy is "complete" joy.

We all know that Jesus faced challenges. Friends betrayed him. People collaborated against him. He was accused in a sham trial and condemned to a brutal death. But listen to what the writer of Hebrews tells us (Hebrews 12:1-3):

> Therefore, since we are surrounded by such a great cloud of witnesses, let us throw off everything that hinders and the sin that so easily entangles. And let us run with perseverance the race marked out for us, fixing our eyes on Jesus, the pioneer and perfecter of faith. For the joy set before him he endured the cross, scorning its shame, and sat down at the right hand of the throne of God. Consider him who endured such opposition from sinners, so that you will not grow weary and lose heart.

Jesus endured the cross because He knew there was joy before Him. He "endured opposition from sinners." You may be dealing with "opposition" during this season of your life. You may have had to persevere through difficult times. I certainly have. And it's painful. But please remember: there will be joy in the morning. Fix your eyes on Jesus. He, too, dealt with opposition from people, but He encourages us to "not grow weary." We are told to "not lose heart."

And let us remember that Jesus persevered because He wanted *us* to have joy. He endured the cross for *us*. He was selfless in His suffering. Yes, He knew He would eventually be back with His Father. But we also know that the night He was betrayed, He hardly slept. And He was in turmoil. Listen to this passage from Luke 22:42-44,

> 'Father, if you are willing, take this cup from me; yet not my will, but yours be done.' An angel from heaven appeared to him and strength-

ened him. And being in anguish, he prayed more earnestly, and his sweat was like drops of blood falling to the ground.

Jesus remained courageous. He kept His eye on pleasing His father. And He remained focused on fulfilling all righteousness.

Consider this insightful quotation from C.S. Lewis:

> It is a Christian duty for everyone to be as joyful as they can be! The entire goal of your life is to glorify God every day that you live. The goal of your life is to honour His Name with every choice you make, every word you speak and every thought you think. You honour God when you choose the joy of His presence. You don't glorify Him through whining, complaining, bitterness or unforgiveness. You glorify God when you choose joy and thankfulness!

I recently communicated with a Christian sister who is suffering, and I shared a passage with her. She knew the passage, and she remembered that her parents used to quote it to her when she faced challenges in her life. It's from 1 Corinthians 10:13,

No test has overtaken you except what is common to mankind. And God is faithful; he will not let you be tested beyond what you can bear. But when you are tested, he will also provide a way out so that you can endure it.

You may be struggling right now. Fear of failure. Financial insecurity. Fear of death. Negative thought patterns. Guilt over sins committed or mistakes made. Workplace challenges. Addictions that seem to rush back with a vengeance.

Don't allow these things to destroy your joy. "That's easy for you to say, preacher." Well, let me put it to you this way. I, too, deal with these things. I, too, must remind myself to stay tapped into the vine. My wife often reminds me that the sermon that I preach will likely be the week's test for me. And oftentimes that observation proves to be very true.

We are in this together. We are all learning. As a congregation, as Christians, we are all walking shoulder to shoulder together. And many of us are wounded. I'm reminded of a war movie where some of the soldiers cannot make progress unless they lean on one of their friends to walk together to safety. Maybe you feel like one of the guys getting carried out on a stretcher! Well, I have news for you. There will be joy in the morning. You can get it back.

This lesson is an important step: *you must stay tapped into the source of true joy*. You must stay connected to the vine. You and I are branches. And we must stay tapped into Jesus, or else our souls will become jaded, darkened, or worse. Only Jesus provides the nourishment that will lead to true, inner joy.

How do you stay connected to the vine? You enter His gates in the morning. You go to Him first thing. You talk to Him in the evening as you lay your head down to sleep. You engage in "ceaseless prayer" throughout the day. Whenever you take a shower, pray to Him. Whenever you see someone in the distance, pray for them.

Pray for the people who need prayer. Pray for your enemies. Pray that God will forgive you for the sins you've committed recently. Ask God to help you be the best person you can be. Ask God to fill you with His joy. Read God's Word. Have fellowship with other Christians. Spend time in the home of God-fearing people. Host godly people in your home. Exchange texts or emails with people you trust, especially if you are going through temptation.

Come to the assembly and rejoice that the Lord died for you and set you free from your sinful past. Be thankful for everything good in your life. Even thank God for the challenges in your life. You need them to grow. You need to overcome obstacles in your life to strengthen your faith. But that requires having obstacles in the first place!

Homework

As we conclude this chapter, I want to ask you to do some more homework. I want you to record ways you will "stay plugged into the vine" this week. What are you going to do to remain plugged in to Jesus? Share your ideas with people—your friends, your family, your church. Be as creative as your heart desires.

This joy stuff is not easy. It requires work. It requires breaking bad habits of thinking. It requires re-training your brain to think Godly thoughts, rather than negative thoughts. You must think like someone who is connected to Christ, rather than someone who has become disconnected from Christ—the true source.

3. Throw Away the List of Wrongs

Let me review what we've done so far in this book.

- In lesson #1, we learned the principle that "you are what you think." If you think about negative things, you'll get negative. But if you think about things that are good, noble, true, pure, and lovely—if you think about those righteous and excellent things—then you'll have more joy. But you must make the choice to clean up your thinking. You have to work hard to prevent your mind from going down into the gutter, down into the darkness. Don't let your thoughts go there.

- In lesson #2, we focused on Jesus, the "true" source of our joy. We focused on Jesus's statement in John 15, that "Jesus is the vine (think about a grapevine), and we are the little branches." If we get severed from the grapevine, then our grapes stop growing. They stay small and bitter. They wither. And that applies to us. If we get disconnected from Jesus, then we wither. We are no longer the good fruit that comes with being connected to the vine.

In this lesson, I want to focus on something that many of us struggle with. Most of us are people of "justice." We want righteousness to prevail. We believe that sins should go punished, and we believe that people should pay for the crimes that they commit.

But we have to remember this—in our *personal* lives, we are commanded, over and over, to forgive. And not only to forgive, but to keep a very short list of wrongs. If we keep on recalling the pain that was inflicted on us, then we live in a damaged state in our minds. If we keep a list of wrongs committed against us, then we live a *paranoid* existence. We lose trust in people. We become cynical. We might even keep a list of wrongs for every single person whoever wronged us:

- He ignored me when it was time for promotion.
- She unfairly accused me.
- He completely misunderstood my intentions.
- She scolded me in front of my family.
- He wrote a humiliating email to me.
- She went behind my back in order to harm me.

He sinned against me many, many times. And now I hate him.

She ignored me for years, and I don't want anything to do with her anymore. That family has never accepted my family, I cannot forgive them for that. My father scarred me when I was a child, how can I ever forgive him for screwing up my life? I will never recover from what he did.

We are hurting. We walk this world wounded. We want justice. Sometimes we crave vengeance. Sometimes we just ignore our trespassers. *We remember*, for better or for worse, and it is painful.

All of that is keeping us from experiencing true joy. We are imprisoned by our own unforgiveness. Jesus showed us how to do it: "Father, forgive them, for they know not what they do." Jesus told us to forgive them over and over. Matthew 18:21-22 says this:

> Then Peter came to Jesus and asked, 'Lord, how many times shall I forgive my brother or sister who sins against me? Up to seven times?' Jesus answered, 'I tell you, not seven times, but seventy-seven times.'

We hold the key to joy. That key is found in forgiveness. It is found in throwing away that list of wrongs committed against you.

The greatest inhibitor of joy in our lives is resentment. I truly believe that. We get upset at someone, and sometimes, we *just can't let it go*.

Resentment separates friends. It separates colleagues. It separates parents and children. It can absolutely destroy your quality of life. And we practice unforgiveness to our own detriment because it goes against everything that Jesus taught us about being His disciples. It robs us of our joy. It robs us of our inner power. We become something that we don't want to become when we're holding on to the sins that people committed against us.

The Lord's Prayer is so crucial in so many ways. Read it and see if you pick up on what Jesus says we should do about forgiveness. Let's look at Matthew 6:9-13. Here's what Jesus said:

> This, then, is how you should pray:
> 'Our Father in heaven,
> hallowed be your name,
> your kingdom come,
> your will be done,
> on earth as it is in heaven.
> Give us today our daily bread.
> And forgive us our debts,
> as we also have forgiven our debtors.
> And lead us not into temptation,
> but deliver us from the evil one.'

Did you catch it? In verse 12, "... as we also have forgiven our debtors." Asking the Lord to forgive our debts is conditional upon us forgiving our debtors.

Further, there is something here you may never have really noticed at all. At the end of the Lord's Prayer, Jesus's mind is still on forgiveness. Out of all of the wonderful themes in the Lord's Prayer: God providing our daily bread, God's kingdom, not falling into temptation, etc... the topic Jesus refers to in the very next verse shows us where his mind was. In Matthew 6:14-15, Jesus says:

> For if you forgive other people when they sin against you, your heavenly Father will also forgive you. But if you do not forgive others their sins, your Father will not forgive your sins.

Love is at the core of the Bible. We are taught that love is what God is. We are taught that the two most important commands in all of creation are love of God, and love of other people. Jesus taught us so many things about *love*. And love keeps no record of wrongs, not even a short one. We are told to keep *no record* of wrongs because that's what a life of love looks like. We shouldn't even keep a "short list" of the wrongs committed against us. We should "forgive" the wrongs committed against us—we should *throw away that list!*

Here's another beautiful way to look at all of this. The apostle Paul says this in I Corinthians 13:4-5:

> Love is patient, love is kind. It does not envy, it does not boast, it is not proud. It does not dishonor others, it is not self-seeking, it is not easily angered, it keeps no record of wrongs.

The path of love is the quickest path to joy. Unforgiveness is toxic and can block all of your joy. If you want joy and happiness and freedom in your life, then *you must personally destroy your desire to hold on to the wrongs committed against you.* You must "keep no record of wrongs."

In the book of Philippians (3:13b), Paul frames this concept another way. It has a similar meaning, but not exactly the same. He talks about "…forgetting what is behind, and straining toward what is ahead."

I have a question for you, and I ask it of myself as well: Why don't we simply forget the negative stuff? Why don't we just let go of it so that we can be the best version of ourselves? I think we all know that we suffer from holding on to negative junk. People insult us, they betray us, and they ignore us. For some unknown reason, we let it stick to us. Why is that? It would be so much smarter, and better for our mental health, if we just put that behind us. Ask yourself this question as you continue reading this chapter: *Why do we hang onto the negative when we'd have so much more joy cutting it off and moving on, not worrying about the things that annoyed or hurt us?*

I think we all *know* that we'd be better off without those negative voices in our heads. But for some reason we choose to keep listening to them, letting them poison our hearts.

At the end of the last chapter, I asked you to do some homework—I asked you to record how you are going to stay plugged into the vine, that is, Jesus. I asked the congregation at Hilltop the same question and received some thoughtful answers. Here are some of their responses:

- One person uses biblical phrases as their computer password in order to keep reminding themselves of the things of God.
- One person listens to Christian radio while driving.

- One person listens to Christian podcasts while exercising.

- One person looks for "glimmers" in life. *What are glimmers?* They are "small moments that make us feel a sense of calm, connection, peace, and safety." Glimmers are the opposite of triggers. Triggers cause stress. Glimmers provide hope and comfort.

- One person is committing to be more *mindful* in their studies of the Bible.

- One person reaches out to 5 people per day to express love and appreciation.

- One person stays connected to the vine by reading the Bible every single day.

- One person simply repeats these words: "I trust you, Lord. It's in your hands. I trust you."

- One person is committing to getting their quiet time routine in the morning going again. They had gotten away from it, but they are going to get back to it, as they realize how crucial it is to stay connected to the vine.

- One person has committed to prayer, each and every morning.

- One person has committed to reading an actual, physical Bible, first thing every single morning.

- One person says they are committed to their life group.

- One person is committed to giving time to our youth group, to help others stay in the Word, and be filled with joy.

- One person is committed to removing curse words from their mouth, as the pain caused by curse words destroys joy.

What a wonderful list. These are things our fellow Christians committed to doing in order to "stay tapped into the vine, which is Jesus," because if we are not plugged in to Jesus, then we will begin to feel the emptiness that comes from being disconnected from Christ.

I realize that you may have been hurt badly. Maybe you were abandoned, or even physically hurt by someone. Some of us carry deep reservoirs of pain. Without minimizing that pain, I want to encourage you to find the strength to forgive. It is the best option for the Christ follower.

As I wind down this chapter, I want to point you to an important scene from the life of Jesus. It is from Luke 23:32-39:

> Two other men, both criminals, were also led out with him to be executed. When they came to the place called the Skull, they crucified him there, along with the criminals—one on his right, the other on his left. Jesus said, "Father, forgive them, for they do not know what they are doing." And they divided up his clothes by casting lots.

Joy in the Morning

The people stood watching, and the rulers even sneered at him. They said, 'He saved others; let him save himself if he is God's Messiah, the Chosen One.' The soldiers also came up and mocked him. They offered him wine vinegar and said, 'If you are the king of the Jews, save yourself.'

There was a written notice above him, which read: this is the king of the Jews. One of the criminals who hung there hurled insults at him: 'Aren't you the Messiah? Save yourself and us!'

The Son of God was insulted. He was beaten. He was betrayed. He was mocked. They spit on Him and hung demeaning signs over His head. They killed Him like one would kill a common thief. Without mercy. And what did Jesus say in response to all this? "Father, forgive them, for they do not know what they are doing."

Forgiveness. But also, grace. Jesus took a gracious view of His killers and mockers. Instead of saying, "They're a bunch of demons," He said, "Father, please forgive them, for they know not what they do." Jesus took a loving and gracious view of all people, even His killers. I know these matters are sensitive and close to the heart, but I want you to at least consider forgiving the people who hurt you badly. Try taking Jesus's view of the situation—that they simply didn't know any better.

You're going to get your joy back if you're able to let all the pain go. If you let the resentment go. If you let the unforgiveness go. If you can start forgiving people, even your enemies, then you can start healing. And every morning, when you rise from your bed, you can have joy, rather than that toxic resentment in your mind. You can enjoy your morning coffee with a smile, instead of anxiety. You can wake up and start praising God for being alive, instead of devoting attention to the ways you've been hurt and wronged in the past.

Homework

Write down the person who you need to forgive most. As hard as it may be, I want you to begin praying for that person. This will be a major step in the direction of joy. Allow yourself to release the pain, so you can begin to feel the joy that comes with forgiveness.

Throw away your list of wrongs. Don't harbor resentment. Throw away the list, and let it go. Free yourself from the shackles of resentment and experience the joy of forgiveness.

4. Suffering Leads to Joy

As we begin the fourth lesson of this book, centered on cultivating joy in your life, I want to encourage you to bring joy to those around you who may not have had so much joy. Visit after church. Invite someone over to your house or to a restaurant for lunch. Make plans to get together during the week. Make someone feel special today. Let's spread the joy to one another.

This book is based on a sermon series I preached at Hilltop titled "Joy in the Morning." The series title comes from a song by Tauren Wells. We played that song and video right at the start and completion of every Sunday service during the series. I hope you'll watch it and get it on your Spotify list. It's a great song that will bring good, wholesome thoughts to you when you listen to it. The inspiration for the song comes from scripture—specifically Psalm 30:1-5. Read this passage:

> I will exalt you, Lord, for you lifted me out of the depths
> and did not let my enemies gloat over me.
> Lord my God, I called to you for help, and you healed me.

> You, Lord, brought me up from the realm of the dead;
>> you spared me from going down to the pit.
>
> Sing the praises of the Lord, you his faithful people; praise his holy name.
>
> For his anger lasts only a moment, but his favor lasts a lifetime;
>> weeping may stay for the night, but rejoicing comes in the morning.

King David wrote this Psalm. He's thanking God. He's praising the Lord for lifting him out of a difficult time when he thought the enemy was going to triumph. He called out to God in his anguish, and God raised him up and led him to victory. He prevented David from being defeated, and David says this beautiful phrase, "Weeping may stay for the night, but rejoicing comes in the morning."

This book is intended to help you develop habits that will lead you to a life of joy.

- In lesson #1, we talked about how important it is to think good thoughts. When we fixate on negative thoughts, we descend into dark patterns of thinking.

- In lesson #2, we listened carefully to the voice of Jesus, who urges us to stay connected to the vine. We are the branches. If we disconnect from Jesus, we wither.

- In lesson #3, we talked about Paul's idea that "love keeps no record of wrongs." Paul and Jesus both urge us to let things go. Forgive people. Don't hold on to a list of wrongs that somebody has committed against you.

I'd like to say a little something about last chapter's homework. As you probably know, the homework I assign to you in these chapters I also assigned to the congregation at Hilltop. When I asked people to text or email me someone they need to forgive, something quite unexpected happened. Crickets. I received very few texts or emails.

Why is that? I wondered. Maybe it was too painful, and they didn't want to confront the harsh memories associated with the person they need to forgive most. Maybe they didn't want the preacher to know who they needed to forgive?! Whatever the case, here are the responses I received, which only a few people completed:

- One person said, "A family member whom I see often."
- One person said, "A parent."
- Another said, "my parents and my sister."
- One person explained that he's not sure if he's quite forgiven two people that he needs to forgive. He prays for them. But he continues to work towards healing and forgiveness.
- One person is struggling to forgive their ex.
- One person needs to forgive their boss.

If you did the homework and centered your thoughts on forgiveness, thank you. I know it is difficult to admit that you need to forgive someone. I hope it was helpful that you were prompted to think of that person and pave a path towards complete healing and forgiveness.

This chapter is about great hope. We are going to talk about suffering and how it often leads to joy in our lives. Sounds weird, huh! But if you are going through something painful right now, if you are suffering, then take heart. Your suffering will lead to great joy if you let God take control of your life.

You may have suffered. Terrible financial losses. Health struggles. Broken relationships.

I have gone through periods of suffering. Some of the stories are too difficult for me to discuss, but as we get farther away from them, they fade a bit and become easier to discuss. I want to tell you a story of when I suffered. It may not seem like a big deal all these years later, but it was a time of true suffering.

In 1999, my wife and I were so happy. I gained acceptance into a PhD program in Canada, at the University of Calgary. It was a major victory in our lives. I've always said the hardest part of a PhD is gaining acceptance into a program. So we packed up and moved to Canada. We loved it. We plugged into a church, and I began a wonderful ministry, serving at the Campbell-Stone United Church. We bought our first house. I was thriving in my new PhD program, and Sunde found a job teaching there. Everything was going so well. I could never bring myself to discuss this publicly, but now, nearly 25 years later, I feel I am able to do so, though it has taken a long time to get to this point, and the scars are still there.

In a PhD program, you are completely under the authority of your supervisor, who is an accomplished professor. That person is called your "doctor father," and they lead you through the program. In the case of Religious Studies, it usually means 5–6 years of doctoral study, after a required 3 years of Master's work!

In my case, my doctor father was a very strict and very scientific historian. There was no messing around, no smiles, no "letting loose," and no joy. His ancestry was German, and he lived up to the German academic reputation. He was extremely overbearing on me. I knew he was shaping me into a true scholar, but I was not prepared for the harsh approach that he took. I looked around at other doctor-father and PhD student relationships, and they were very different. Some professors gave their office keys to their PhD students and let them use their personal libraries. They'd go out and eat together. My experience was not like that at all. My supervisor would go so far as to shout at me in public, which happened on one occasion.

Now keep in mind that Sunde and I were in Canada on a student visa. I had to be enrolled, or else I would have to leave the country. We were immigrants. We had no special coverage by the government. All we had was my student visa.

One day, my supervisor came to my graduate desk and asked me to come to his office. He asked me about my foreign languages. I told him that I had a year of German and two years of Greek, which he knew. I told him that I had met with the graduate coordinator, who told me that my language component had been fulfilled.

And my supervisor said, "Frankly, I disagree." That completely caught me off guard. I did not understand where the anger was coming from, but something had set him off. He dismissed me back to my desk.

A few minutes later he came back to my desk and asked me to come to his office again. When I walked in, he said, "Dyron, you're not my student anymore. I'm not going to supervise you anymore. You're on your own. So long."

The department was very humane with me. They allowed me to remain enrolled as a student, so Sunde and I wouldn't have to leave the country. The department knew I was a good teacher, so they had me teaching round the clock. I taught a lot of courses for them. I had played my cards right and made myself useful. I had established good relations with other professors, especially with the Head of the Department, who kept giving me teaching opportunities.

But, boy, I was in a state of depression, anxiety, and suffering. I had no supervisor. I was no longer studying because it wasn't clear what I was to do. After a few months, I formally approached another professor to supervise me, so I could continue on with my PhD, but he declined. He said he just didn't have the bandwidth. I had horrible thoughts of returning to the USA with my tail between my legs. "There's Dyron … the guy that went to Canada to get a PhD but failed. He got thrown out of his program, and out of the country."

The department had every right to say, "Sorry, Dyron … it just didn't work out. We're going to have to unenroll you from the program." I was hanging by a thread.

Trying to keep people on my side, so they didn't sever me from the university.

It was a disaster. Really brutal. I remember one night, Sunde and I watched the movie Cast Away. It is still one of my favorites. But that movie summarized my life. I felt alone. Lost. Cast away. Rejected. And I had no power to get my life back on track.

You may have watched that movie and had a different understanding of it than I did. But it fit me perfectly. I was destroyed. Broken down to my bare soul. My dignity was shattered.

Then at the end of the movie, you may not even remember, Tom Hanks' character is standing at a cross-roads—literally a cross-roads out in the country. Standing at that juncture, he looked this way, and then that way. He didn't know which way to go. His life could go in one of four directions. When the movie finished, the floodgates opened. I began weeping and crying, with deep aching inside of me. Sunde didn't understand. But I wept and wept. I had hit rock bottom, and somehow that movie summarized everything I had felt.

Then, one day shortly after that, I got into my car. It was in the middle of winter, with deep, deep snow all around. I had walked a long way, probably a mile, from the university to the parking lot. I was freezing, and I felt defeated. I turned on my car and just sat there, thawing out. You know how the heater goes—the air is cold for the first five minutes or so, and then eventually it starts warming up. So I just sat there and prayed. "God, please help me. I am lost, O God. I am at the end, O Lord. If you are out there, Lord, I need you to help me right now. Because I don't know how long I can stay in this situation, God."

Then I turned on my radio, and you won't believe what happened. It was a Christian radio station. A song came on that, amazingly, I had never heard before. The artist's name was Riley Armstrong, and he sang a rendition of a song that you probably know—"Like a Bridge Over Troubled Waters." I know it now, but that night in 2001, I had never heard the song.

It's hard to believe, but when I called upon the Lord and turned on my radio that night, God responded to me with those lyrics. I was stunned. God spoke to me that day, and I've never forgotten that moment, nor that song.

Eventually, one day, my supervisor and the head of the department talked to me and explained the situation. Remember, I was in the dark as to what I did wrong, but it was explained to me that my supervisor wanted me to take another foreign language. Of course! I was happy to do that. But come to find out, he was *really* upset at the fact that the graduate coordinator told me I was done with foreign language, when in fact my supervisor wanted me to take another year of foreign language.

Can you believe it? That was it! That's what all the pain, all of the uncertainty, all of the fear and failure... it was just about that. We humans get so angry about such little things.

What do we make of that story? I learned three things:

- God is with you. He's paying attention.

- God uses our suffering to teach us lessons. He doesn't cause the suffering, but he uses it to equip us for greater things.

- God will bring joy out of the sorrows. Joy will come in the morning. You just have to be tenacious and long-suffering. Joy will come.

I look at my life now. I have a wonderful family. I have my church family. I have work that I love and enjoy. I have plenty of food. Many friends. I have four children who show me such tenderness, love, and respect—so much more than I deserve. I have parents who love me deeply. I am so blessed.

But that deep, dark valley shaped me. It humbled me. It broke me down. It showed me that when everything is taken, you still have a God who loves you, who walks with you daily, and who, yes, communicates with you.

Dear friends, the apostle James wrote these powerful words (James 1:2-4):

> Consider it pure joy, my brothers and sisters, whenever you face trials of many kinds because you know that the testing of your faith produces perseverance. Let perseverance finish its work so that you may be mature and complete, not lacking anything.

I want to ask you to do something right now... Remember that *God is producing something good in you.*

When you know that God is producing something good in your life, even in the most challenging times, *it brings great joy*. Do not give up or grow weary. Joy is coming, and Jesus will give you the strength to endure whatever hardship you are going through right now. I would like to end this chapter with a reflective task for you.

Homework

Describe the most difficult time of your life. You don't have to go into detail as I did, but document that experience as authentically as you can. You can summarize it in a sentence or two. Then try to find some kind of joy that came out of that trial or that difficulty. James says to "consider it pure joy when you go through trials," but oftentimes we don't easily recognize the lessons we've learned through those trials. That's your homework. Search for the good lessons that came out of your suffering, and seek joy in those lessons you have learned.

In closing, remember this—you must go through these kinds of things in order to grow. And growth is to be celebrated because when you get through the trial, you have gained. You have learned. You have benefited from experience.

We've all come through dark valleys. But we've also learned that those valleys don't last forever. There will be joy in the morning.

5. Don't Become Bitter

Overview of the lessons so far:

- In lesson #1, we talked about how important it is to *think good thoughts*. When we ponder negative things in our minds, then we descend into dark patterns of thinking.

- In lesson #2, we must *listen carefully to the voice of Jesus*, who urges us to *stay connected to the vine*. We are the branches. If we disconnect from Jesus, then we wither.

- In lesson #3, we talked about Paul's idea, that "*love keeps no record of wrongs.*" Paul and Jesus both urge us to *let things go*. Forgive people. Don't hold on to a list of wrongs that people have committed against you.

- Last chapter, lesson #4, we discussed how *suffering often leads to great joy*.

In this chapter, we're going to talk about why you should channel your efforts into combatting bitterness. Bitterness will lead you to all the wrong places, at least mentally.

Before we dive into the subject matter, I would like to speak briefly on last chapter's homework. If you completed it, thank you for doing so. It is difficult to recall painful experiences—just as I did in the last chapter about my former supervisor. However, it is vitally important that we look back to see how far we've come and *joyously celebrate* the fact that we survived the storms.

I assigned the congregation at Hilltop the same homework, to document their painful life events. Here's what some of them wrote:

- I struggled to find a spouse for years. Now, we've been married for 15 years and have two beautiful children.

- I had a divorce after many years of marriage. Many scars are still there. But I remarried a true Christian person, and have used my experiences to minister to others.

- My brain surgeries were hugely challenging. But now I have raised a lot of money for brain research, and great things have resulted.

- The loss of a bad relationship led me to the right school, which brought me into a good relationship, and into a beautiful marriage!

- I was in a job that was dangerously bad for me, so I left. Within two weeks, God put me into the job of my dreams—where I have been serving joyfully for 28 years now.

- My childhood was tough. But I'm still working through it by working on myself. I'm learning how to have compassion on others, and I continue to serve the Lord with everything I got.

I deeply appreciate these folks sharing their stories. I am thankful that we all can celebrate the joy God gives us as we emerge from difficult times.

Today, I want to talk with you about a concept that can truly help you keep your joy: "*Don't Become Bitter.*" If you get bitter, you're going to probably have more bad days than good days. You're going to see the worst in your daily tasks. You'll resent your boss and your work. You'll distrust the people around you. Your quality of life will plummet.

A few years ago, I had a private conversation with a high-level administrator at Pepperdine. I have known this fellow for years—I even knew his father! This man almost always has a smile on his face. As an administrator, he's surrounded by problems much of the time. Stressful job. Huge responsibilities. Yet he smiles and shakes hands as if everything is great.

During that conversation, I asked him how he did it. "How do you stay so positive and joyful all the time," I asked him. "What's your secret?" And here was his answer: "Don't become bitter."

Bitterness is bad for you. It is bad for organizations. It is bad for churches. Read this verse from Hebrews 12:14-15,

> Make every effort to live in peace with everyone and to be holy; without holiness no one

> will see the Lord. See to it that no one falls short of the grace of God, and that no bitter root grows up to cause trouble and defile many.

The lesson? Don't become the bitter root that causes trouble in a church or an organization. If you keep at it, then you will "defile many" others.

Ephesians 4:31 is another important Bible verse dealing with bitterness:

> Get rid of all bitterness, rage and anger, brawling and slander, along with every form of malice. Be kind and compassionate to one another, forgiving each other, just as in Christ God forgave you.

Bitterness is particularly toxic because it spreads like a contagious disease. If you are sitting at a dinner where everyone is gossiping or talking ill of something or someone, the tendency is to partake. Bitterness can grow up in people-groups, and can undermine organizations, teams, and families.

Back when my wife was teaching at a Mennonite elementary school in Canada, she went to the faculty lounge one day and a bunch of the lady teachers were sitting there talking about how bad their husbands were. One lady would say, "Oh you think that's bad, let me tell you about my husband … he hasn't washed his clothes in weeks." Another lady would come along and say, "Aw, you think that's bad, my husband doesn't lift a finger to help me with dishes, even after I cooked the meal." And on and on.

My wife walked in and, for some reason—thanks be to God—she was feeling good towards me that day. She walked in and said, "Oh, my Dyron, he often does the dishes, and when he does the dishes, man, they are clean! And my Dyron is a very clean person. He picks up after himself, and keeps his closet orderly."

You could have heard a pin drop. And what happened next? The ladies all turned and looked at my wife. Then they kind of glanced at each other a bit. One lady spoke up then, saying, "Well, *my* husband makes the best steaks you've ever tasted." Another chimed in, "Well, you think that's good; *my* husband takes the kids out once a week so I can have some alone time!" Another spoke up, "My husband is awesome ... sometimes when he's out for a run, he brings in flowers from the garden for me."

Just like *that*, a *bitter root* turned into a *sweet-smelling rose*.

What's the lesson here? Don't allow somebody else's bitterness ruin your perspective. And if things begin to go that way, you can be the one to freshen up the conversation with positivity and joy. You can literally change the entire situation with your words. You can become infected by bitterness, or you can spread joy and grace.

Once, Wendi Gilchrist sent me a YouTube link featuring an interview with a psychology professor from Stanford named Jamil Zaki. Professor Zaki wrote a book called *Hope for Cynics* that I bought after watching the interview. At the beginning of the book, this professor begins by talking about his research. He researches concepts like kindness, empathy, and having faith in one another. However, as he confesses on page 1, he's lived his life with a dirty little secret: he's actually very cynical. He says this, "In private, I'm a cynic, prone to seeing the worst in people." He goes on to explain that when he was a child, he had a very chaotic family life. He learned to distrust people.

He's lived with great tension. His research always told him that compassion is much better for us than selfishness. Donating money literally activates good chemicals in your brain. Helping other people with their problems actually calms us down. In spite of this, Zaki only saw this information as his *research*. Deep down, he didn't view people very favorably, probably due to his painful childhood.

Throughout the book, the professor talks at length about the power of hope. He discusses the perils and pitfalls of gossip, and how it can make us really bitter and distrustful. He talks about how we can rebuild trust in each other, even in a nation that seems to be divided. He reminds the reader that the world will become what we build. We can build a cynical world, where everyone looks like a monster to each other, or we can build a trusting, hopeful world, where we see everybody as having potential.

At the end of the book, he says that he still has dark moments. In fact, he laments the fact that over time, cynicism became his "default mode." It festered and made him bitter, but writing this book was therapeutic for him. As a scientist, he began to see that the data kept coming back in favor of virtues like hope, compassion,

Joy in the Morning

and altruism. He realized that he was seeing the worst in people by choice, rather than looking for the good in people. You find what you look for in others. If you are looking for the bad in people, you'll find it! If you're looking for the good in others, you'll find that, too! The question is, "Which one do you want to look for?"

He confesses that he hasn't turned positive and hopeful overnight. No, it is a work in progress—but there is progress. Near the end of the book, he writes, "New habits of mind and action are taking root. Trust is growing more natural. ... Hope has never been foreign to me, just forgotten."

In the Bible, when armies would go to war with one another, the best way to overtake a city was to clog up its wells so it had no access to fresh water. Armies would throw big stones into the well to the point where the water would shut off from inside. In Genesis 26, we find a fascinating story about Isaac—the son of Abraham. Isaac's men were at war with the Philistines, and the Philistines used this tactic—they threw stones into Isaac's wells to the point where there was no water.

I have a question for you. Has your well of joy been stopped up by something? Has life thrown stones of disappointment into your well so that joy doesn't flow anymore? Is there someone in your life who, every time they come around, throws another stone into your well, plugging up your joy? Maybe you are clogging up your own well of joy by focusing on your mistakes, or by expecting perfection from yourself or the people around you—like your children.

In Genesis 26:18-25, we read a fascinating passage:

Isaac reopened the wells that had been dug in the time of his father Abraham, which the Philistines had stopped up after Abraham died, and he gave them the same names his father had given them.

Isaac's servants dug in the valley and discovered a well of fresh water there. But the herders of Gerar quarreled with those of Isaac and said, 'The water is ours!' So he named the well Esek because they disputed with him. Then they dug another well, but they quarreled over that one also; so he named it Sitnah. He moved on from there and dug another well, and no one quarreled over it. He named it Rehoboth, saying, 'Now the Lord has given us room, and we will flourish in the land.'

From there he went up to Beersheba. That night, the Lord appeared to him and said, 'I am the God of your father Abraham. Do not be afraid, for I am with you; I will bless you and will increase the number of your descendants for the sake of my servant Abraham.'

Isaac built an altar there and called on the name of the Lord. There he pitched his tent, and there his servants dug a well.

Have you become bitter? Are your wells clogged? Did someone throw rocks into your well of joy? Perhaps you neglected the well and, over time, silt and stones collected inside, obstructing its flow. Maybe you clogged your own well of joy.

However those stones got there, I want to encourage you to get to work. Get down in there and start removing those stones. That's what this book is for. It's supposed to motivate us to get to work, so we can unclog those wells and get joy flowing again. Those stones and all that silt is making you bitter. You can't drink water from a stopped up well—it becomes rancid and bitter! You've got to get down there and work to unclog it.

What does this mean for you?

- Maybe you need to stop blaming other people for everything.

- Maybe your cynicism is destroying your joy.

- Maybe you fill your mind with bad news—climate catastrophes, political infighting, controversies, etc.—to the point that you've clogged up the joy wells!

I want to encourage you to find ways to unclog your wells. Get that joy bubbling up again. Allow that fresh water into your soul. There's one sure way to do it, too. In John 4 there's a wonderful and inspiring story about —you guessed it—a well. Jesus went to this well to get some water, and he encountered an outcasted woman there: a Samaritan (whom Jews typically hated). Jesus asked her for a drink. The woman protested because Jesus was a Jew and she was a Samaritan. But Jesus used this moment to teach her a lesson that is now world-famous:

John 4:13-14

> Jesus answered, 'Everyone who drinks this water will be thirsty again, but whoever drinks the water I give them will never thirst. Indeed, the water I give them will become in them a spring of water welling up to eternal life.'

Dear reader, Jesus is the source of your joy. He offers living water that will not only fill you with joy, but will well up to eternal life within you.

To access the living water of this well, you must remove the silt and stones that are blocking it. Is it resentment? Have you given up the battle to fight against your cynicism? Like Professor Zaki from Stanford, you've got to keep trying. You don't want to end up cynical and bitter. You've got to keep working at it. Keep trying to find the good in people. Look for it. Because you'll find whatever you are looking for.

Homework

What is blocking your joy well? What is preventing you from having fresh water flowing up from within you, rather than bitter, undrinkable water? Looking back at your childhood, has something rooted within you and made you grow bitter?

I have two questions for you:

1. What's blocking your joy?

2. What can you do to unblock it and get your joy back?

I ask that you reflect on these questions and preserve your thoughts in writing. As we conclude this chapter, let's review a few thoughts from Professor Zaki on cynicism and how to overcome it:

> Cynicism is an understandable response to a world full of injustice and inequality. But in many cases, it is misplaced. Dozens of studies find that people fail to realize how kind, generous, and open-minded others really are. Cynical thinking deepens social problems: when we expect the worst in people, we often bring it out of them. We don't have to remain stuck in this cynicism trap.

Jesus Christ can help you unclog your joy well, but you have to invite him to help you. A stopped well, with enough elbow grease and patience, can once again produce life-giving water. Approaching your well with humility, forgiveness, and love, as Jesus would, and reigniting love and hope for yourself and others goes a long way in revealing the everlasting spring of joy in you.

6. Choose Your Companions Wisely

In this chapter, we will be discussing *why you should choose your companions wisely*.

Here are a few Bible verses to soak in before we plunge into this chapter's content:

- Proverbs 13:20: Walk with the wise and become wise, for a companion of fools suffers harm.

- 1 Corinthians 15:33: Do not be misled: "Bad company corrupts good character."

- 2 Corinthians 6:14: Do not be yoked together with unbelievers. For what do righteousness and wickedness have in common? Or what fellowship can light have with darkness?

- Psalm 141:4: Do not let my heart be drawn to what is evil so that I take part in wicked deeds along with those who are evildoers; do not let me eat their delicacies.

- Proverbs 22:24-25: Do not make friends with a hot-tempered person, do not associate with one easily angered, or you may learn their ways and get yourself ensnared.

Those are some powerful verses, and they're not always easy to follow. Some of us are very close with unbelievers. Some of us work with people that could be considered "bad company." We can't just switch jobs. Some of us are hot-tempered by nature. We come by it honestly. Maybe we grew up with a parent who was hot-tempered, so we ourselves have become hot-tempered. Therefore, some of us may find ourselves in a difficult situation: we want good, Christian friends, but as soon as they discover our "hot temper," they start ghosting us. Why? Because they don't want to become tainted by all the drama that our hot temper brings.

There is another major issue at play here. We are animals. Sometimes we get caught up in a crowd and we start behaving badly. As animals, we tend to feel safer whenever we are acting the way the people around us are acting. And if those people are acting badly, our tendency is to act badly. This is sociology 101.

And then that passage on being "yoked with unbelievers." It's a famous passage. There again, we are animals. We may enjoy the company of someone who does not share our Christian beliefs. Or, perhaps when we are young and not so serious about our faith, we date non-Christians. Or we end up as close friends with a circle of people who do not really live for God, and we develop good friendships. It's not that they're bad human beings … it's just that they don't share the same first love that we share as Christians: we are in love with Jesus, first and foremost.

I once heard the saying that "You are the average of the five people you spend the most time with." I suspect there is a grain of truth in that. Another version of that saying is that "Your life is the average of the five people that you have spent the most time with up to now."

"Bad company corrupts good character" is what the Bible teaches. However, there are exceptions to this idea. For example, Jesus himself spent time with sinners in order to extend grace to them, or to mentor them. So please don't get the impression that God's Word teaches us to only hang out with people who share our values. I think the Bible is teaching us that our most primary "companions" should be godly people. Choose your inner circle carefully. Choose who you date carefully.

I often remind my own children, "You marry who you date." Of course, a typical teenage response is, "I'm not necessarily going to marry the person I date as a teen." But I did. My wife and I started dating as teenagers, and we got married young. There is also a very strong likelihood that your marriage will not be an arranged marriage. In other words, you will marry the person you date. It may not be the first person you ever date. But it might be.

Think with me for a moment. Who do you spend the most time with? Who are the five people you spend the most time with? Is it your family? Or do you spend more time at work than you do with family—and sleep time doesn't count!

This can be a sobering thought. Maybe you spend a few hours with your family each night ... but how much time do you spend with your co-worker who sits in the next cubicle? Maybe it's a fair estimation that you are the average of the five people you spend the most time with.

Now, what does all of this have to do with joy? In other words: *What does our companionship have to do with joy?*

I think there are three ways to answer that question.

"A companion of fools suffers harm."

If you hang around foolishness, you're going to bring harm on yourself. I'm reminded of the many scandals that have been in the news the last few years. We'll often hear about how a person's life became wicked and corrupt, and then we see pictures of a certain celebrity or politician hanging out with that person. By spending time with that wicked or corrupt person, those celebrities and politicians suffer harm to their own reputations.

The title of this chapter is "choose your companions wisely." If you somehow find yourself in the company of fools, the Bible's advice is to get out! Run for the door. You can excuse yourself by saying, "Excuse me, I need to make a phone call." Or you can simply excuse yourself to the bathroom and think of a way out of the situation. But, flee you must. You can't afford to be under the influence of wickedness and foolishness.

Sometimes foolishness is not so easy to recognize. For instance, if you find yourself in a conversation that is full of gossip, you need to get out of it. Read what the apostle Paul says about a group of young widows he was having to deal with in 1 Timothy 5:13-15:

… They get into the habit of being idle and going about from house to house. And not only do they become idlers, but also busybodies who talk nonsense, saying things they ought not to. So I counsel younger widows to marry, to have children, to manage their homes and to give the enemy no opportunity for slander. Some have, in fact, already turned away to follow Satan.

You see, whenever we allow ourselves to get drawn into these destructive conversations, not only do we damage someone else's reputation, we also damage our own hearts. These are people we're talking about. They have families. They are God's children. They are people with dignity.

If the group that is gossiping consists of Christians, then name it for what it is. You can say something like, "Friends, we should stop talking this way. Let's repent and ask God to forgive us for gossiping. Jesus says, *Do unto others as you would have them do unto you*. None of us want others to gossip about us. So let's not gossip about others."

Here's Proverbs 20:19: A gossip betrays a confidence; so avoid anyone who talks too much.

Proverbs 17:4 says: A wicked person listens to deceitful lips; a liar pays attention to a destructive tongue.

Again, if you find yourself on the receiving end of gossip, slander, or conversation unfitting for a Christian, then either gently and politely stop the conversation, or find a way to excuse yourself—so you don't end up bringing judgment upon yourself.

A companion of fools will suffer harm, and harm will bring the opposite of joy.

Now back to our question:

What does our companionship have to do with joy?

Good companions will lead you to good, positive conversations.

Good, positive conversations will lead you to much more joy. If your companions are positive, caring, and full of wisdom, then you are going to have much more joy in your heart. You are going to be a beneficiary of their goodness, of their joy, and of their ability to uplift you.

Paul says the following in Colossians 4:6, "Let your conversation be always full of grace, seasoned with salt so that you may know how to answer everyone."

Ephesians 4:29 says the following: "Do not let any unwholesome talk come out of your mouths, but only what is helpful for building others up according to their needs, that it may benefit those who listen."

Proverbs 16:24 says the following: "Gracious words are a honeycomb, sweet to the soul and healing to the bones."

Too often in life, we find ourselves having conversations that are negative. They can even be self-defeating. Let's be honest here, who wants to hang around somebody who just constantly brings us down? Who wants to be companions with someone who is always criticizing everyone? Here's the catch, according to the Bible–
–If you hang around those folks long enough … you'll

start acting like them, talking like them, and being just like them. So flee from those downer conversations and choose friends who lift your soul and speak goodness and positivity into your life.

Now, the third way to answer the question: *What does our companionship have to do with joy?*

We're not looking for perfection in our friends. We're looking for disciples of Jesus.

Before we get too demanding in how we can choose companions wisely, let us remember that we are imperfect. None of us are perfect, and none of us deserve perfect friends. We are all imperfect people with hang-ups, with mistakes in our pasts, with annoying little habits, and with problems that most people probably don't want to hear about.

So what is my point? My point is that we should not expect our companions to be perfect.

We should, however, absolutely strive to create a circle of companionships devoted to Jesus. In our opening Bible passages, we are instructed on some aspects of what our companions should be like. Here's what we are told:

- Walk with wise people. Hang out with fools and you'll bring self-inflicted harm upon yourself.

- Bad company corrupts good character.

- While it is important that we interact with non-Christians, our inner circle should be filled with disciples of Jesus Christ.

- Get too close to wicked people, and you'll find yourself doing wicked things.

- Avoid hot-tempered people. They can "ensnare" you with their zero-to-sixty temper.

Now, here's a question. What if you're the hot-tempered one of the group? What if you're the one leading folks to gossip or to be negative? What if you're the person who tends to bring the conversation down, or to inject it with controversy and unhealthy emotion?

If you're that person, then you need to repent. You need to ask for forgiveness. You need to admit to yourself that *you* are sometimes the problem. If that's us, then we need to take the steps to confess our sin, commit to doing better, allow ourselves to be accountable to our friends, and change our conduct.

Nobody wants to be abandoned once they're caught sinning, so we're not expecting perfection here. We're expecting discipleship, and that's very different from perfection. Discipleship means you're trying. You are committed to Jesus, and while you will make mistakes, you are still working hard to live a life that is in step with Jesus.

Dear reader, if you do these three things:

- Choose your companions carefully;

- Be careful about your conversations; and

- Look not for perfection, but for disciples ...

Then you are going to have more joy in your life. You'll have more joy in your relationships. Instead of getting caught up in the latest negative news, or gossip, or doomsday idea ... you'll focus on how to bring humor, happiness, and positivity into your life.

Be the kind of person who injects goodness and joy into your conversations. That's the kind of person we all should want to be like. And those are the kinds of people we all need in our lives.

Homework

I'd like you to do something very simple. I would like you to estimate where you and your companions' conversations rank on a scale of 1 to 10. If your conversations are pretty much negative all the time, you should give yourself a 1. If you and your companions' conversations are excellent and wholesome all the time, then give yourself a 10.

Try to be honest with yourself. We are doing this because it is important to self-reflect and commit to putting in the work to improve our conversations and ultimately bring about more joy in our lives.

To close, I ask that you choose your companions wisely. Commit to being a good companion to those who love and trust you, too. Surrounding yourself with Christ-centered companions and uplifting conversation is a sure-fire way to beget joy.

7. Be a Generous Person

This chapter examines *why it is important to be a generous person.*

However, before we begin talking about generosity, I'd like to share the Hilltop congregation's self-evaluations, which you were prompted to complete in the last chapter. As a reminder, the task was to rate your conversations with your companions on a scale of 1 to 10, with 1 being mostly destructive and 10 being mostly wholesome. Here are some of their statistics:

Our final score was 6.0. We had 27 respondents. We had no 10 scores. We had one nine and a couple of 8 scores. But our average was exactly 6.

In other words, we have room to grow when it comes to the conversations we are having with the people around us. Let's all work hard to season our conversations with grace. Let's try to speak positively with the people around us. Let's keep the negativity, the gossip, and the "woe is me" talk to a minimum.

Of course, there are times when we need to talk with someone about something that is bothering us. But we don't have to think about that stuff, and talk about that stuff, all the time. Let's try to occupy our conversation with positives:

- Instead of negative comments about someone, replace it with positive comments.

- Instead of putting ourselves down, let's build ourselves up.

- Instead of choosing to talk about worrisome, discouraging news with our companions, let's choose to focus on positive and hopeful topics.

Instead of getting up in the morning and talking about the latest political news, get up in the morning and talk about what God is doing in your life. Let's study the Bible first thing in the morning and pray to the Almighty about what we hope to accomplish that day. That will set our minds in the right direction. And it will shape the ideas that come out of our mouths.

Now ... let's talk about how to become a more generous person.

I'd like to spend the first part of this chapter looking back at the Old Testament. I have two stories in the Old Testament that I think impactfully illustrate how God wants us to think about generosity. The two passages are found in Deuteronomy 15 and 1 Chronicles 29.

The first story, found in Deuteronomy 15, is when the Israelites were commanded to cancel each other's debts. This startling passage instills fear in the hearts of any banker or creditor!

> At the end of every seven years you must cancel debts. This is how it is to be done: Every creditor shall cancel any loan they have made to a

fellow Israelite. They shall not require payment from anyone among their own people because the Lord's time for canceling debts has been proclaimed. You may require payment from a foreigner, but you must cancel any debt your fellow Israelite owes you. However, there need be no poor people among you, for in the land the Lord your God is giving you to possess as your inheritance, he will richly bless you, if only you fully obey the Lord your God and are careful to follow all these commands I am giving you today. For the Lord your God will bless you as he has promised, and you will lend to many nations but will borrow from none. You will rule over many nations, but none will rule over you.

If anyone is poor among your fellow Israelites in any of the towns of the land the Lord your God is giving you, do not be hardhearted or tightfisted toward them. Rather, be openhanded and freely lend them whatever they need. Be careful not to harbor this wicked thought: "The seventh year, the year for canceling debts, is near," so that you do not show ill will toward the needy among your fellow Israelites and give them nothing. They may then appeal to the Lord against you, and you will be found guilty of sin. Give generously to them and do so without a grudging heart; then because of this the Lord your God will bless you in all your work and in everything you put your hand to.

> There will always be poor people in the land. Therefore I command you to be openhanded toward your fellow Israelites who are poor and needy in your land.

Isn't that fascinating? Every seven years, the Lord required the Israelites to cancel the debts of whoever owed them. The motive was so that there would be no poor people. The spirit of generosity would lead to blessings from God— generosity leads straight to God's blessings. With a generous spirit, you would get to the point where you would "lend, not borrow."

God commanded them to not be "tightfisted." Rather, he commanded them to be "openhanded." They were not to resent this seventh year, either. It was a violation of the spirit of this law if they tried to get around it. God commanded them all to "give generously," and not with a grudging heart.

If they followed God's advice on this, then he would bless them in all their work and in all that they would do … "in everything you put your hand to."

The final verse is a passage that Jesus actually reiterates in Mark 14. In that passage, Jesus says, "The poor you will always have with you." In Deuteronomy, it reads, "There will always be poor people in the land."

Why are we analyzing this passage in the Old Testament? It is because we see the long history, the long trajectory that goes way back to ancient times connecting generosity with God's blessings. It is an important concept in the Bible, and it helps to see how long this concept has been around.

Similarly, we turn to 1 Chronicles 29. The context here follows David trying to get people to be generous so that they can build a temple—the Jerusalem temple. King David asked everyone to give generously, and they did. The leaders really stepped up and gave with all of their hearts, and David was impressed. In this passage, David gives thanks to God for all of the generosity among God's people. Notice how this reading actually ends with the concept of *joy*.

> 1 Chronicles 29:6-17
> Then the leaders of families, the officers of the tribes of Israel, the commanders of thousands and commanders of hundreds, and the officials in charge of the king's work gave willingly. They gave toward the work on the temple of God five thousand talents and ten thousand darics of gold, ten thousand talents of silver, eighteen thousand talents of bronze and a hundred thousand talents of iron. Anyone who had precious stones gave them to the treasury of the temple of the Lord in the custody of Jehiel the Gershonite. The people rejoiced at the willing response of their leaders, for they had given freely and wholeheartedly to the Lord. David the king also rejoiced greatly.
>
> David praised the Lord in the presence of the whole assembly, saying,
>
> 'Praise be to you, Lord,

the God of our father Israel,
> from everlasting to everlasting.
Yours, Lord, is the greatness and the power
> and the glory and the majesty and the splendor,
> for everything in heaven and earth is yours.
Yours, Lord, is the kingdom;
> you are exalted as head over all.
Wealth and honor come from you;
> you are the ruler of all things.
In your hands are strength and power
> to exalt and give strength to all.
Now, our God, we give you thanks,
> and praise your glorious name.'

'But who am I, and who are my people, that we should be able to give as generously as this? Everything comes from you, and we have given you only what comes from your hand. We are foreigners and strangers in your sight, as were all our ancestors. Our days on earth are like a shadow, without hope. Lord our God, all this abundance that we have provided for building you a temple for your Holy Name comes from your hand, and all of it belongs to you. I know, my God, that you test the heart and are pleased with integrity. All these things I have given willingly and with honest intent. And now I have seen with joy how willingly your people who are here have given to you.'

What do we learn from this passage? We learn that the leaders stepped up and gave big, which encouraged the entire community to give big. We learn that the Israelites sacrificed in order to build a temple unto the Lord. We learn that David "rejoiced greatly" (v. 9) when he saw the "willing response of their leaders."

We also see here a theology of giving, a theology of generosity. It is all based on our adoration and respect for the Lord. Our giving comes out of our dependence upon God. David asks, "Who are we?" He points out that our days on earth are "like a shadow." Like the book of James teaches, we are like "mist," here one day, and gone the next. Everything we have comes from God. Our abundance belongs to God. We certainly don't take it with us. As David says, everything comes from God, and we only give what has already come from God's hand because it all belongs to God anyway.

I also love how David is careful that he and his people give with "honest intent." David points out that God "tests the heart." There are times where God tests our hearts on this issue of generosity. And in this case, the Israelites gave willingly, and with integrity.

There is a wonderful passage on this concept of God testing. God tests our hearts, but He also invites us to test Him when it comes to generosity. The passage is from Malachi 3:10:

> 'Bring the whole tithe into the storehouse, that there may be food in my house. Test me in this,' says the Lord Almighty, 'and see if I will not throw open the floodgates of heaven and

pour out so much blessing that there will not be room enough to store it.'

There is this back-and-forth concept with God when it comes to our generosity. We give to the Lord, and we give to others ... but we trust God, that he will replenish us. We know in our hearts that we serve a good God, and He will take care of all of our needs. This concept gave David great joy. His people were so willing to give to the Lord, with great trust in their hearts that God would reward their generosity. This all made David so joyful that he celebrated by leading the community in worship to God, and in prayer to the Lord.

The theme of generosity continues into the New Testament as well. Let's now read some of the most important New Testament passages that deal with being a generous person.

> 2 Corinthians 9:6-8
> Remember this: Whoever sows sparingly will also reap sparingly, and whoever sows generously will also reap generously. Each of you should give what you have decided in your heart to give, not reluctantly or under compulsion, for God loves a cheerful giver. And God is able to bless you abundantly, so that in all things at all times, having all that you need, you will abound in every good work.

In that same passage, the apostle Paul says this little verse to summarize his teaching on generosity:

> 2 Corinthians 9:11
> You will be enriched in every way so that you can be generous on every occasion, and through us your generosity will result in thanksgiving to God.

The other famous passage from the apostle Paul on the topic of generosity comes from his first letter to Timothy, the young pastor he was mentoring. Here's what Paul said to Timothy in 1 Timothy 6:17-19:

> Command those who are rich in this present world not to be arrogant nor to put their hope in wealth, which is so uncertain, but to put their hope in God, who richly provides us with everything for our enjoyment. Command them to do good, to be rich in good deeds, and to be generous and willing to share. In this way they will lay up treasure for themselves as a firm foundation for the coming age, so that they may take hold of the life that is truly life.

Our Lord and Savior, Jesus Christ, also taught us to be generous people. Here are a few of the passages that Jesus gave regarding giving to others and being generous:

- Acts 20:35b: It is more blessed to give than to receive.

- Matthew 6:1-4: Be careful not to practice your righteousness in front of others to be seen by them. If you do, you will have no reward from your Father in heaven. So when you give to the needy, do not announce it with trumpets, as the hypocrites do in the synagogues and on the streets, to be honored by others. Truly I tell you, they have received their reward in full. But when you give to the needy, do not let your left hand know what your right hand is doing so that your giving may be in secret. Then your Father, who sees what is done in secret, will reward you.

- Matthew 6:19-21: Do not store up for yourselves treasures on earth, where moths and vermin destroy, and where thieves break in and steal. But store up for yourselves treasures in heaven, where moths and vermin do not destroy, and where thieves do not break in and steal. For where your treasure is, there your heart will be also.

- Matthew 10:42: And if anyone gives even a cup of cold water to one of these little ones who is my disciple, truly I tell you, that person will certainly not lose their reward.

- Luke 6:38: Give, and it will be given to you. A good measure, pressed down, shaken together and running over, will be poured into your lap. For with the measure you use, it will be measured to you.

- Luke 21:1-4: As Jesus looked up, he saw the rich putting their gifts into the temple treasury. He also saw a poor widow put in two very small copper coins. "Truly I tell you," he said, "this poor widow has put in more than all the others. All these people gave their gifts out of their wealth; but she out of her poverty put in all she had to live on."

Dear reader, let us be generous people. This is an old truth that goes back to the very origins of our faith—back to the Old Testament. And it is a time-tested truth. When we give to God, when we give to the poor, when we trust God to replenish our generosity, it is then we are showing our great trust in God. He is our father. He takes care of us. Over and over in the Gospels, Jesus teaches His listeners to trust in God, and not to worry about finances. God will take care of us just as he takes care of the lilies of the field and the birds of the air.

What is absolutely true in all of this is that you cannot outgive God. God will pay you back, and you will be amazed by His generosity.

A joyful heart is a generous heart. When you give to help people, or when you give to help a cause, you are emulating God. That's why it feels so nice. The endorphins rush into your veins because you are giving something that is valuable to you. You are giving to God, or to someone who is poor, or to a good cause. It is a step of faith, but it is a step of faith that comes with many benefits, including joy and satisfaction in your heart.

Homework

I'd like to ask you to put a dollar amount to how much God has blessed you in this life. Estimate, in dollars, how much God has given to you. And when you do that, ponder the generosity of God.

8. Don't Panic. Turn to God.

This chapter has to do with something we've all dealt with: anxiety. Or, as we call it here: *panic*. Some of us struggle with it more than others, but I hope this material will be a good reminder that God is faithful, and He provides us with tools from His word that will help us to panic less and turn to Him more.

Before we begin the lesson, let's look at how Hilltop responded on the topic of generosity. As you'll recall, I asked you to think about how much God has blessed you in this life, and I asked you to put a dollar value on it. I didn't receive a lot of answers, but I did receive a few. Of those responses, we are talking—at least—*millions of dollars for each person*. In fact, several congregants said, in essence, that your blessings exceed money. God has showered us with so many blessings that it exceeds dollar values: a spouse, children, eternal life, loving friends and a loving church, and more. How do you assign a dollar value to so much?

I'm reminded of a conversation I had with a previous Provost at Pepperdine—the Provost is the person in charge of academic operations at a university. We were in his car, driving down the PCH, and I asked him how much the land at Pepperdine is worth.

Pepperdine is located on prime real estate in Malibu. It consists of 830 acres, on a bluff and a mountainside, overlooking the Pacific Ocean. According to Zillow, the average price of a house in Malibu is $3.5 million. That's actually a bargain, compared to the $200 million house that Beyonce and Jay-Z bought in Malibu in 2023. Their house set a record—which lasted about one year, as someone bought a house for $210 million *this* year.

So, I asked Provost Tippens how much the Pepperdine land was worth. His response reminded me of the old Mastercard commercial: "priceless." I asked Dr. Tippens what he meant. I told him everything has a dollar value... doesn't it? He said, "No." Actually, the 830 acres there in Malibu will only rise, stunningly, over time. There is absolutely no point in trying to assign a value to it because by the time you find a buyer, the price has already risen by millions.

Plus, why would you want to leave that beautiful location? Location-wise, it only goes down from there. In other words, nobody in their right mind would sell that land. It's just too valuable. It exceeds money.

Initially, I was shocked by Provost Tippens' response, but it is similar to what some wrote to me in their responses. Some things exceed finances. Money pales in comparison to the value of my children, my life, my faith, or my freedom. These are things that exceed all the money in the world! Like the Pepperdine property—money falls short! Now, let's pivot to the concept of panic. I want to begin with a hypothetical story. Let me know if you can relate.

I had a good weekend. Church was great on Sunday. I got to connect with my brothers and sisters in Christ. I feel safe at church. True friendships. Great people. A very high level of trust.

Then... Monday happens. I go to work with a smile on my face. I'm thinking about the "Generosity" sermon. I'm focusing on my life in Christ and how many blessings I've received. I'm so fortunate to be a disciple of Jesus. Happy, happy, joy, joy.

Remember, it's Monday. I walk into my office. Two colleagues come up to me and ask me questions that I cannot answer right away. I need to think about them for a while, but they're pretty important questions that need an answer soon. As Billy Joel, Queen, and David Bowie all sang: *PRESSURE!*

Then I open my emails. One of them says, "No" to something I requested. And the "no" was not sugar-coated. It was a pretty stark "no."

So, then I need to make an important phone call. It doesn't go well. The person on the other end is clearly not happy with something. So, I try to work the situation out, but it's awkward. I hang up the phone, knowing that conversation didn't go well. Happy, happy, joy, joy is no longer there.

Got another email from my boss asking me to get something done more quickly than I was expecting. "Okay. Of course I'll get it done!" (Gulp! Really? Why did I just commit to that?)

So, I go pick up my mail in the Religion office area and walk right by someone with whom I had a disagreement recently. She doesn't even look at me, despite the fact that there is no one else in the room. We just kind of walk right by each other. Silently. I'm trying to smile at her, but she won't even look up. *AWKWARD!*

Then I receive a text—someone I care deeply about is not doing well at all. Very serious health issues. I need to get a flight to go see them. Or should I stay home so I can put out all of the fires at work and finally get caught up?

Oh, by the way, the boss was supposed to meet with me but just cancelled on me. Why did he do that? What's the problem? I heard about cutbacks, but why would he just cancel a meeting like that… with no explanation? Very uncharacteristic of him.

Okay, okay. You get the point. Can you relate to *any* of that?

Sometimes panic sets in. We get overwhelmed. The week did not kick off the way I was expecting it to. Then I open God's Word and read this challenging—but very soothing—passage (Proverbs 3:5-6):

> Trust in the Lord with all your heart
> and lean not on your own understanding;
> in all your ways submit to him,
> and he will make your paths straight.

The title of this chapter is "Don't Panic. Turn to God."

I can assure you that very soon—probably this week, and possibly tomorrow—you're going to start your day with panic rather than with peace, calm, serenity, and joy.

But here's the good news. *It is within your power.* You have control here. You cannot control other people. But you CAN control your response to other people.

- You CAN gather your bearings before you send an offensive or abrasive email to someone.

- You CAN collect yourself when someone tells you "no." You can breathe deeply and strategize your next move. Are you going to accept the "NO"? Or are you going to think of a way to get around that barrier? When you've rested and thought about it, maybe you will have more creative responses.

- You CAN pray before your phone calls. You CAN put a Bible verse (the one we just read) in front of you on a piece of paper or on a screen to look at WHILE you're talking to the person on the phone. That will keep your head in the right place.

- You CAN pray fervently for your friend. You CAN Zoom with your friend if you simply cannot get away from work. Or, you can humbly approach your boss and explain the situation… and go see your friend who is struggling with health issues.

- You usually CAN explain to your boss that you will work hard on that task he needs on his desk tomorrow. But you can let him know that both you and he will get better results if you can have until the end of the week, or even over the weekend, to get it done.

- If your boss screams, "*Of course not!*" Then you CAN go back to your office, fall on your knees, and ask God to help you learn how to pray for your enemies!

- You CAN give it a few days and circle back with your boss and say, "No problem about us not meeting last week, but I'm available this week for a meeting, if you are."

> Trust in the Lord with all your heart
> and lean not on your own understanding;
> in all your ways submit to him,
> and he will make your paths straight.

When we panic, we are *far* less likely to make the right decision. When we panic, we are *far* less likely to be our best self.

The only time panic helps you is when you're confronted by a bear.

Wait! My family was confronted by a big bear this summer… and we DIDN'T panic. Rather, we kept our cool. Well, Ross filmed it. When Ross panics, he likes to film. But the rest of us just kind of kept our heads. The girls prayed. I must confess I took some pictures, hoping they were not the last pictures ever taken of our family. "The Daughritys sure were a nice family. Look, here are the last four photos of them ever taken before they were eaten by bears."

Dear reader, don't panic. Rather, seek God. We need to *turn to Him*. Don't allow your panic to force you into a bad decision. Don't allow panic to steal your joy.

Joy in the Morning

Don't allow panic to set in. Stop and pray. Seek God. Trust in the Lord with all your heart. Don't lean on your own understanding of the situation because your understanding is very limited. In ALL your ways, submit to God, and he will straighten out this mess. He will straighten out your day for you. Panic is only going to make things go south.

Before writing this chapter, I looked up the word "panic." I'm very interested in etymology, the study of the history of words. You want to know where the word "panic" comes from? It actually has its roots in two Greek words. The first is "pan," which means "all" or "everywhere." Think of words like "panorama," which means "all – view." (The word "horama" means "view.")

But where does the word "pan" come from? The word "pan" is actually the name of a Greek God. Read this fascinating explanation from Merriam-Webster's dictionary:

Panic comes to us from French *panique*, which in turn derives from Greek *panikos*, meaning literally "of Pan." Pan is the pipe-playing, nymph-chasing Greek god of fertility, pastures, flocks, and shepherds. He also has a rather dark side — his shout is said to have instilled fear into the giants who fight with the gods. The Greeks believed he was responsible for causing the Persians to flee in terror at the battle of Marathon. Panic entered our language first as an adjective, suggesting the mental or emotional state that Pan was said to induce. The adjective first appeared in print at the beginning of the 17th century, and the noun followed about a century later.

And what does the word "panic" mean now? Here is a good definition of the word from Oxford Languages: "A sudden, uncontrollable fear or anxiety, often causing wildly unthinking behavior."

How many of you have panicked recently? Did you run in circles out of anxiety? Did you lose your temper at your child because you lost control for a moment? Did you get fearful about something and run off and do something irrational?

I'm sure most of us did. Sadly, panic is a human response. It is a fear response, and it gets us into trouble sometimes. Today's lesson is going to help you overcome it.

If you don't know, I am a big fan of Rick Warren. I read his devotionals daily. Not too long ago, he had two lessons on panic, and he gave excellent advice on how to fight against it. Here were his suggestions of what you should do whenever you are tempted to panic:

- Don't panic, get the facts.
- Ask for more time.
- Gather prayer partners.
- Ask God for supernatural help.
- Worship God.

Using the story of Daniel, Pastor Warren tells us that there is a formula for dealing with panic. And here it is:

Joy in the Morning

Get facts, ask for more time, pray with people, turn to God, worship God.

Finally, I want us to read the KEY scripture in the Bible that tells us how to deal with panic. It is found in the incredibly powerful book of Philippians, written by the amazing apostle Paul. Here is that verse, from Philippians 4:4-9.

> Rejoice in the Lord always. I will say it again: Rejoice! Let your gentleness be evident to all. The Lord is near. Do not be anxious about anything, but in every situation, by prayer and petition, with thanksgiving, present your requests to God. And the peace of God, which transcends all understanding, will guard your hearts and your minds in Christ Jesus.

Finally, brothers and sisters, whatever is true, whatever is noble, whatever is right, whatever is pure, whatever is lovely, whatever is admirable—if anything is excellent or praiseworthy—think about such things. Whatever you have learned or received or heard from me, or seen in me—put it into practice. And the God of peace will be with you.

Let's end this chapter by breaking this passage down into digestible instructions:

- Rejoice *in the Lord!*
- Be gentle with people.
- Know that God is very near.

- Pray, don't panic.

- Put your head into a space of gratitude.

- In every situation, pray.

- Think about very, very positive and holy things. Don't let your mind spiral into negative patterns. Don't think bad thoughts about people. Don't go there mentally.

- Think about how the apostles handled themselves in the Bible. And then, "Do what it says." Do what the apostles say we should do. Follow their lives and teaching in Acts and in the Epistles—that's where you'll get apostolic instruction.

If you follow that passage of scripture carefully, you will not panic. You will have peace. God will come near to you, and you will be able to rejoice with him. Remember, the word "rejoice" is based on the word "joy."

Do you want more joy? Then learn how not to panic. Rather, learn how to turn to God during those difficult moments of anxiety.

Homework

For your homework, I request that you identify one piece of advice from God's word—perhaps one we analyzed in this chapter—to internalize and focus on this week. You probably don't have the scriptures memorized, but you *can* remember one of these messages from scripture to put into practice, to help you to overcome the temptation to panic.

We all want peace. Because it's hard to have joy without peace. So please ponder at least one thing you can do from this chapter—from God's word—that you can put into use this week.

Let us be people of *joy*, not people of panic.

Let us learn to turn to Him, rather than allow our minds to go into a frenzied state.

Let us worship God now and purge our minds of stress. Let's sing out to Him with worshipful hearts and experience the inner peace He will provide for us.

9. Joy is Medicine for the Soul

I have a friend who told me recently that he only has good days. I asked him how he manages to do that. He said every day is a gift, and he makes sure that every single day is a good day. He said you squander it if you let the day get ruined. It's up to each of us which direction the day will go.

Today's lesson is called "Joy is Medicine for the Soul." In this chapter, we're going to back up just a bit and analyze *why* it is that we're trying to get to a place of joy in our lives. We just have four more chapters in this book, so as we enter the final stretch of this journey of joy, let me ask you—has this book helped you to think more deeply about your joy, or your lack of joy, or the obstacles you may have to joy? Perhaps this book gave you some ideas for what you need to work on in order to have more joy in your life?

Personally, I have found these lessons to be difficult but extremely rewarding if I actually put them to work in my life. I think we all know that when Jesus is in our lives, we will have more joy. That's why the "Vine and the Branches" lesson was so important. Perhaps it was the most important of the book because if we are not connected to Jesus—the true vine—then it's all for naught.

If we are not connected to the Source, then we won't have the kind of joy that the Bible calls "the joy of the Lord." You might laugh, you might have some happiness, but "the joy of the Lord" is different. It is stable. It is life-sustaining, even during difficult times. The joy of the Lord is true joy.

I was reading about definitions of joy this week, and of course there are many. Most of them include words like "pleasure" and "happiness." However, the more thoughtful definitions come from Christian authors who understand the concept of "the joy of the Lord." And the concepts that they include in their definitions often have to do with *surrender and transformation*.

In other words, if you are seeking the joy of the Lord, then you'll have to *surrender* to the Lord. You'll have to give Him your life and your burdens, and you'll have to make Him your priority. You must surrender to God. That's the first concept of Christian joy that we must internalize.

The second key concept has to do with *transformation*. True joy means that you are being transformed by God. He is making you more like the person He wants you to be. He is molding and shaping you, like a potter does with clay. In fact, that is an analogy that the Bible uses: God is the potter, and we are the clay.

We surrender to God. We become clay in His hands so that He can shape us into the person that He wants us to become. We must surrender our will, knowing that God's version of us is far superior to any version of ourselves we or anyone else might contrive. Some of us have tried to do it alone, without God, and it didn't go so well. But with God molding and shaping us, we become better. We become filled with His Spirit. We become close family members with the Church—the home of God's people. We also become happier, and full of God's joy. Our sadness becomes less than our joy because we are living the life that God wants us to lead.

When you become like clay for God, he will shape you—and he will also use you to accomplish His purposes. He will use your life to bring others to Him—to reconcile other people to Him. It is a beautiful process, and it includes much joy because when we are being shaped by God, and God is using us for His kingdom purposes, then we become our best selves. Full of joy.

Now, whenever you begin to walk in step with the Lord, you will be constantly re-energized by His joy. It will heal you. It will be like balm for your soul, like medicine for your heart and mind.

The Bible puts it this way (Proverbs 17:22, NASB):

> A joyful heart is good medicine,
> But a broken spirit dries up the bones.

Did you get those two concepts? Joy is like medicine to us. It provides healing. When our heart is joyful, we are improving. We are getting better. We are being made whole—on the up and up.

However, whenever our spirit is broken, we become spiritually and mentally dry and worn out. We become brittle, unable to move well. We become weakened and fragile—an inferior version of ourselves.

The bottom line is that with joy, you will be a better version of yourself. Thus, each of us should strive to have more joy in our lives, which means we should work on the weak areas of our lives that are blocking our joy. With joy, our hearts are merrier, we have a bounce in our step, and we will be better for the people around us—our families, our coworkers, and our friends.

By the way, scientific studies have shown that good relationships are crucial for longevity and a higher quality of life. Some of you may have heard of the "Harvard Study of Adult Development." It is one of the best and most reliable studies of longevity in existence. It is supported by the National Institutes of Health, among other important agencies. It began in 1938 when Harvard researchers started studying male Harvard sophomores to see which ones lived happier and healthier lives. President John F. Kennedy was one of the original recruits.[1]

Over time the study expanded, and they included the men's offspring. It has expanded several times over the years, and the data that is being collected is wonderful. Naturally, they found that good genes play an important role in longevity and happiness. They also found that taking care of your body is important. I think we all know these things—not much new information there.

---

[1] See "Good genes are nice, but joy is better," *The Harvard Gazette*, 11 April 2017, located at: https://news.harvard.edu/gazette/story/2017/04/over-nearly-80-years-harvard-study-has-been-showing-how-to-live-a-healthy-and-happy-life/.

The surprising data revolved around the area of relationships. People who have good relationships with their family and friends are far more likely to live long, and to be happy. This surprised scientists. "Close relationships," is how they defined it. When you are tied to people, you are protected from the "discontents" of life. Close relationships help to ward off cognitive decline. In fact, let me quote a line from an article I read about this study. It says,

> "Close relationships ... are better predictors of long and happy lives than social class, IQ, or even genes. That finding proved true across the board among both the Harvard men and the [later] inner-city participants."

Here's another passage:

> "Researchers who have pored through data, including vast medical records and hundreds of in-person interviews and questionnaires, found a strong correlation between men's flourishing lives and their relationships with family, friends, and community. ... The people who were the most satisfied in their relationships at age 50 were the healthiest at age 80."

Sounds like, once again, God's Word has been proven by science:

> A joyful heart is good medicine,
>   But a broken spirit dries up the bones.

The Harvard study has shown that those who have close, warm relationships live longer, have more joy, and rarely experience loneliness. This is where it gets ugly—the study also included these lines: "Loners often died earlier. Loneliness kills. It's as powerful as smoking or alcoholism."

There is one more thing about this study that I want to share with you. Your "close relationships" don't have to be perfect. Read this insight from the Harvard study:

> "Good relationships don't just protect our bodies; they protect our brains… And those good relationships, they don't have to be smooth all the time. Some of our octogenarian couples could bicker with each other day in and day out, but as long as they felt that they could really count on the other when the going got tough, those arguments didn't take a toll on their memories."

What's the point here? The discovery they have found is that you don't have to have the perfect relationship with those people whom you consider to be in "close relationship" with you. You can have ups and downs. You can go through hard times. You can even bicker every day. But if you have a connection, and a commitment to one another, then you are going to live longer, have more joy, and be healthier.

It is important that we have joy in our lives. Being joyful has all sorts of benefits. It will help our relationships, it will help our own biology, it will improve our mind and emotions, and it will protect us from cognitive decline. Joy is the glue of our relationships.

Let me add another important piece here that I learned from Pastor Rick Warren. He says this:

> "The basic law of relationships is this: You tend to become like the people you spend time with. If you spend time with grumpy people, you get grumpier. If you spend time with happy people, you get happier."[2]

As discussed a few chapters ago…*you* need to be happy, partly so that the people around you are happier. You don't want to be the thorn in the side of the person you love. I don't want Sunde or my kids to get sad or deflated every time I get home, or whenever I interact with them. I want people to be happy that I'm home… happy that I enter the room… happy that I stand up before them to speak at church. I want to be happier and more joyful, partly so the people in front of me will be happier and more joyful.

I have read studies where they say smiles cause dopamine to be released in our brains. So you actually have the power to give people a dopamine hit when you smile at them! Imagine that, you can give dope to other people! Just smile at them!

---

[2]Rick Warren, "Pride Destroys, Humility Builds," 31 October 2024, located at: https://pastorrick.com/pride-destroys-humility-builds/.

But seriously, don't allow your face to be downcast. Put your thoughts on the things above, and you'll have more joy and more hope.

Psalm 42:5 states,

> Why, my soul, are you downcast?
> > Why so disturbed within me?
> > Put your hope in God.

Colossians 3:1-2 states something similar:

> Since, then, you have been raised with Christ, set your hearts on things above, where Christ is, seated at the right hand of God. Set your minds on things above, not on earthly things.

In other words, change your thinking. Think about God. Think about good things. Think about all that you have received in Christ Jesus. This will make you smile more. And when you smile more, you release more dopamine, both to yourself and to the person you smile at!

The famous "joy chapter"—Philippians 4—gives us instructions on how to think well. Heed these words:

> Finally, brothers and sisters, whatever is true, whatever is noble, whatever is right, whatever is pure, whatever is lovely, whatever is admirable—if anything is excellent or praiseworthy—think about such things.

So, what are you going to think about? Are you going to think about negative stuff? Are you going to think about fear, and all of the reasons you should be scared? Are you going to think critical thoughts against your spouse and loved ones?

NO! Of course not! If you want to have joy, health, and longevity, then think about admirable and lovely things. It's your choice. It's up to you how much joy you want in your life. You have to make the decision to think better thoughts.

Homework

For your homework, I want you to speak to the people you have "close relationships" with. I want you to tell them how much you love them, how much you appreciate them, and how much you want to grow old with them. Tell them that you are "better together." Let them know that you don't ever want to be isolated, so you look forward to growing closer together for the rest of your lives.

Dear reader, you should know in your heart that your relationships are going to help you physically, mentally, and spiritually for the rest of your life. Know that your life is likely to be a long and healthy one if you honor those people who are close to you—if you treat them well. Because remember, the closer you get with those folks, the more joy, mental health, and longevity you will experience.

Oh, and one more thing … DON'T FORGET TO SMILE AT EACH OTHER!

We could all use a little more dopamine!

10. Joy is Found in Community

With this chapter, I want to discuss how we find joy in community.

Let's start with a question. Do you come from small-town America? I do. I grew up in a little place called Portales, New Mexico. When I was growing up, it was a town of 12,000 people. Still today, it remains a town of about 12,000 people.

I didn't realize it at the time, but what I had in that small town was beautiful. Most people either knew each other or were just one step away from everyone. If you didn't know someone, then you surely knew someone who knew that person. It was like a web, and everyone was connected.

But in that town, and in my growing up, I experienced *true community* in that little church where I went at least three times a week. In those days, we went to church on Sunday morning, and we hardly ever failed to return on Sunday evening at 5pm for another service. We also had Wednesday night Bible classes that felt compulsory. You didn't *have* to go to the Sunday night or the Wednesday night services, but there was a core of people who did.

How many of us grew up in this kind of church setting?

My family and I truly felt like we belonged to the Southside Church of Christ. There were probably 200 attendees on a Sunday morning, and we all knew each other. We knew every single person. We knew what everyone did for a living. We knew where everyone was from, and what everyone's kids had done once they graduated from high school.

Don and Shirley Shultz were a wonderful couple who taught me Bible Class in the upstairs classroom when I was little. Thom Moore was always quick to tell me a joke. Marlin and Frank Poynor were brothers from Texas and businessmen, who had settled down in Portales to start a business that did quite well. Jack Self—a close friend of my grandfather—was the superintendent of the children's home that my grandfather started. Jack's son, Rod, succeeded him in that role. Rod was also my teacher for Sunday School when I was in high school. Rod and I used to play tennis together.

Jake Taylor was a brilliant psychologist who clearly had a heart for God. Emmitt Clayton led the best prayers, and they always began with "Dear Lord, we come to you with thanksgiving in our hearts." I still remember that. Sweet Emmitt died while underneath his car when he was probably in his early sixties. He had it jacked up and was fixing something—as you did in those days—but the jack gave out and the car crushed him. It was tragic. Emmit's wife, Joanne Clayton, was my 2nd grade teacher in the public schools, and I'll never forget what she wrote on one of my report cards.

She said, "Dyron is my little ray of sunshine." I've never forgotten that.

Bill Turnbow was my dad's best friend. He died a couple of years ago while on a bicycle race in the mountains of Colorado. He was in excellent health, and was in his late 70s. My dad has never been the same since Bill died. My father is an extreme introvert, and Bill was the only person he did things with. Losing Bill dealt a devastating blow to my family.

Emil Johnson was an elder in the church, and he was a great woodworker. He made the cupboards at our church. He was a quiet man, but always kind. Kind of gruff. His voice always sounded like gravel was in it.

Jan Casey was so fun. She was a good friend of my mom. Her husband died many years ago. After her husband died, Jack Self's wife also died—lo and behold, they were always at church worshipping together. They began to talk a lot after church, since they were both alone, and eventually, they got married! It was surprising to everyone, but their marriage lasted probably 15 years! She died recently in a car accident with her husband Jack in the car beside her. He was injured and was unable to return home, so he is now in a rest home in Lubbock.

And so it goes. If you were part of a small town, a tightly-knit church, then you know exactly what I'm talking about. All of these people have lives that intersect in so many ways. They interact at potlucks, at each other's homes for special events, they watch the Super Bowl together, they give gifts to each other's kids. They all stepped up and pooled their money when we expanded our church building. They all mourned when my grandfather died—as he was the founder of that church. There is now a playground behind the church called "Grover C. Ross Park."

We are living in a very different world today. We don't return to fellowship and worship together on Sunday nights, nor do we come here on Wednesday nights. We do still have other opportunities to gather. We get together on Saturdays sometimes. We go to each other's homes. We have Life Groups, where people can get really close and tightly-knit into each other's lives, sharing burdens, and rejoicing in each other's milestones.

I have mixed emotions about those "good ole days." I don't live in a quiet, small rural town on the plains of New Mexico. It took us, literally, about 4 minutes to drive from our home to the church—which was clear on the other side of town. My life is now in a huge city. It takes some of us half an hour to get to church. We travel for work. We have so many things to do. Life has gotten *so busy* in the last 40 years.

And, of course, the ubiquitous cell phone pulls us away from one another. Families sprawl around on couches in the evening, but everyone is on a separate device. One person is getting caught up on work stuff on their laptop. Someone else is in a texting conversation. Someone else is watching cooking videos on their I-pad. Someone else is playing a game on their Kindle. These devices. Boy, these devices. They have changed us in so many ways. I must confess to you …. It is very difficult to manage four children and their time on de-

Joy in the Morning

vices—especially now that three of my kids are nearly adults.

It's not that my family is uniquely bad. I think we are typical in the sense that these devices have kind of taken over our lives. Email. Games. Text. Internet access, with virtually every newspaper and magazine at our fingertips. The phone is a television, a movie theater, a calendar, a travel agent, a shopping cart, and so much more, all rolled into one!

What do we do in a world that is so busy, so full of devices, and so disconnected, polarized, fearful, and suspicious?

This is the antidote: you find a community. You stick with them. You commit to them. You live life with them. You get frustrated with them sometimes. You disagree with them occasionally. But you eat with them a lot. You share your heart with them from time to time. You attend baby showers with them. You go to funerals with them. You celebrate when someone gets a new job. You try to help someone who is going through a rough spell in life.

It's called the church. And it was created by God. Why did God create this community? So we could have joy. So that we could experience the joy of community. Of growing old together. Of hearing the Word of God preached. It's a place where you celebrate Jesus Christ together and grow in your faith with one another.

I've often heard college students and others say something like this: I love Jesus, but I do not like the church. Sometimes they'll put it this way: I have faith in God, but I've lost my faith in the church.

My question is this: How do you lose faith in your family? You don't lose faith in your family. You may go through ups and downs, but you eventually work it out. Don't harbor ill will. Learn how to forgive. Learn how to sit next to someone who thinks a little differently than you.

Most congregations have differences among them. Different races. Different political affiliations. Different age groups. Different education levels. Totally different jobs and hobbies.

But we have each other. We have our unity in Christ.

Read what Paul wrote in Philemon 1:7. He said this: "Your love has given me great joy and encouragement because you, brother, have refreshed the hearts of the Lord's people."

Joy and encouragement. Those are two of the big reasons people gather in churches. To celebrate a new baby, or the coming holiday season. The church is growing—perhaps a congregants just got baptized on Sunday!

We also encourage one another. Some of us are fighting through pain every Lord's Day. Back pain. Knee pain. Arthritis. And there's also heartaches that we experience in this life: broken relationships. Kids moving away. We have sins that we struggle with, and make us feel bad about ourselves.

That's why we come to church. To encourage each other. To make each other feel like normal people when we come together. To shake hands and hug and pat each other on the back. To introduce ourselves to new faces. To feel dignity at church.

I'm sorry, but I don't like it when people say, "I've lost faith in the church." The solution is not to lose faith in each other. The solution is to work through things together. The solution is to continue to love and encourage one another, even if we aren't exactly the same in every way! Hear these tender words from Paul in the book of Philippians:

> It is right for me to feel this way about all of you, since I have you in my heart and, whether I am in chains or defending and confirming the gospel, all of you share in God's grace with me. God can testify how I long for all of you with the affection of Christ Jesus. (1:7-8)

While I don't like to dwell on the COVID-19 pandemic very much, I feel it is appropriate to discuss here. During that horrible time, churches were unable to be together. Some of us got very sick, and we all know people who passed away. We were confused because even the experts didn't fully understand the disease, or what to do about it. So, we all just sat in our homes and stared at screens, watching each other on Zoom. Some churches divided. Many people simply walked away from the church during that time. When we all started going back to church in 2021, we realized that so much had changed.

Here is another tender word from the apostle Paul in Philippians 2:1-4:

> Therefore, if you have any encouragement
> from being united with Christ, if any comfort
> from his love, if any common sharing in the
> Spirit, if any tenderness and compassion, then
> make my joy complete by being like-minded,
> having the same love, being one in spirit and of
> one mind. Do nothing out of selfish ambition or
> vain conceit. Rather, in humility value others
> above yourselves, not looking to your own in-
> terests but each of you to the interests of the
> others.

Paul experienced great joy in the Christian community. He gave his life to establishing churches all over the Mediterranean region. Paul told his congregation to value one another. Consider the dignity of one another. Put other people's needs ahead of your own. Don't be selfish. Try to find the unity that brings us all together. Paul calls this "joy."

Some of the best advice Paul ever gave to the church can be found in the letter to the Romans 12:10-18:

Be devoted to one another in love. Honor one another above yourselves. Never be lacking in zeal, but keep your spiritual fervor, serving the Lord. Be joyful in hope, patient in affliction, faithful in prayer. Share with the Lord's people who are in need. Practice hospitality.

Bless those who persecute you; bless and do not curse. Rejoice with those who rejoice; mourn with those who mourn. Live in harmony with one another. Do not be proud, but be willing to associate with people of low position. Do not be conceited.

Do not repay anyone evil for evil. Be careful to do what is right in the eyes of everyone. If it is possible, as far as it depends on you, live at peace with everyone.

None of us are perfect. So don't give up on your church, your family. Rather, grow together. Rejoice together. Mourn together. Grow in your faith and grow as a family in Christ.

Let us spend more time in fellowship with one another, and less time in isolation, on our screens, becoming resentful of the world.

Jesus created the church. He called it His "bride." The "Bride of Christ." This concept is found in Ephesians, 2 Corinthians, and Revelation. We are His bride. The church is important, and God wants you to be part of it because that is the best place for you to grow closer to Him. Hear His Word, watch how others are growing in their faith. Make yourself helpful to the people around you. Find a way to contribute. Give. Receive. Enjoy. Rejoice.

This is our family! This is our church building where we can gather and have fun and worship God together!

In the last chapter we explored the famous Harvard Study on the quality of human life. One of the biggest takeaways was that social isolation is worse than alcoholism or smoking. It can literally kill you. You can become so lonely that you become terribly unhealthy.

My friend, the church can help with that. We are a body. We are a family. We need each other badly. Our families need each other. The latest converts to the faith, the newest baby, the newest members—they all need you.

You are needed. We all need each other.

The title of this chapter rings with so much truth: Joy is found in community.

Homework

For your homework, I hope you will commit to doing one thing this week with someone from your church. Coffee. Lunch. Evening together. That's your homework. Enjoy another person, or another family, in your church. Because it's YOUR church. And, above all, it is Christ's church. It is His bride. And we are truly privileged to be a part of this community.

11. The Joy of Heaven

With this chapter, we begin to wrap up this book titled "Joy in the Morning." The key idea of this book has been that if you start your day with God, then you are likely to experience His joy all throughout the day.

This lesson has to do with the "Joy of Heaven."

I would like to start by sharing a song with you. You may know it, or you may not have heard it before, but I am nonetheless excited to share it with you. The song is by a Christian music group called Mercy Me, and is entitled "I Can Only Imagine."

If you watch the music video, you might ask, "What's up with all the picture frames?" Well, the inspiration for the video came from people at Mercy Me concerts who started holding up empty picture frames during the song "I Can Only Imagine." They were doing this to pay tribute to their loved ones who had passed on. The video was kind of designed as a "shout out" to the fans who came to their concerts and started doing this little ritual.

Later in the video, the people start showing actual pictures of their loved ones who have gone to be with the Lord. It is painful to watch and to think about, but, in a strange way, it is also very encouraging. Especially when you consider the lyrics that are being sung in the background by Mercy Me.

This beautiful song, clearly about Heaven, has touched so many lives since its release in 1999. It hit #1 on Christian radio and was the most played Christian single in 2002. It also won "Song of the Year" for the 2002 Dove Awards. It crossed over into the secular charts as well, as so many people found hope in it—that perhaps their loved ones are in heaven with Jesus.

In 2018, a film was released about the story behind the song. The film's title is the same as the song's title: "I Can Only Imagine." When the film came out, the single hit #1 again. It has been widely praised as one of the greatest songs ever written in the history of Contemporary Christian Music. It is the most played song ever in Christian radio history, and is by far the best-selling Christian single of all time. It has gone platinum five times in the United States alone.

The song was written by Bart Millard, the lead singer of Mercy Me. He said he wrote it in five minutes, as the words just poured out while he was mourning the death of his dad. Millard was only 19 years old when his dad passed away from cancer, and this song represents his deep grieving, as well as his deep faith that his father would be with Jesus, in Heaven, surrounded by His glory.[3]

---

[3] See Wendy Lee Nentwig, "Song Story: 'I Can Only Imagine'," 26 September 2003, located at: https://web.archive.org/web/20120403075437/http://www.crosswalk.com/church/worship/song-story-i-can-only-imagine-1221889.html.

One of the most interesting things about this song is that the songwriter, Bart Millard, was not in a good place financially when the song came out. His father had actually set up an annuity for his two sons just before his death. That annuity would pay the sons a little bit of money for ten years, to help them along as they started their adult life. Perhaps it is irony, or perhaps it is more than irony, the song "I Can Only Imagine" hit #1 on the radio the same week that his father's annuity ran out. The success of the song guaranteed Bart would have enough to sustain himself... plus some!

The people holding up pictures in the video all have a story to share. For instance, one of the women, Tammy Trent, holds up a picture of her husband who died in a diving accident. The picture she holds up was captured just 30 minutes before his accident. He's sitting on the boat that he dove off. But she said it would be an honor for her husband's picture to be in the video. She then said, "I never leave the house without that song since he died."[4]

As I write this, I am dealing with two separate issues that are pretty heavy. One of my faculty members at Pepperdine lost his mother. He was hurting badly, as he loved her deeply. At our faculty meeting on Tuesday, I asked him how he was doing, and he said, "About like you'd imagine right now." He had actually just spent some time with his mother in Texas the week before, but shortly after he returned to California, she passed on to be with the Lord. He had some lectures he needed to

---

[4] Nentwig, cited above.

give, and he needed to get a few things done before he headed back for the funeral. I did my best to offer my comfort to him.

On another note, one of my former students, Brian Craig, also passed away this week. He was almost exactly my age. He was a minister at a church, and was one of the most positive and grounded students I have had in my career. He was so kind and respectful towards me, despite our similarity in age, and he made a huge impression on me. He developed brain cancer and had been kind of fluctuating health-wise for several years. At a church leader's retreat last week, he fell and had a seizure from which he never recovered. Brian was a musician and wrote and performed Christian music that was picked up by churches all around the world. His music will continue for a long time. It's his legacy.

The apostle Paul wrote these hopeful words when contemplating the resurrection of Jesus, as well as our own resurrection from the dead, in 1 Corinthians 15:51-57:

> Listen, I tell you a mystery: We will not all sleep, but we will all be changed—in a flash, in the twinkling of an eye, at the last trumpet. For the trumpet will sound, the dead will be raised imperishable, and we will be changed. For the perishable must clothe itself with the imperishable, and the mortal with immortality. When the perishable has been clothed with the imperishable, and the mortal with immortality, then

the saying that is written will come true:
"Death has been swallowed up in victory."

"Where, O death, is your victory?
 Where, O death, is your sting?"

The sting of death is sin, and the power of sin is the law. But thanks be to God! He gives us the victory through our Lord Jesus Christ.

Indeed, we can only imagine what Heaven will be like. We do have some passages in the Bible that give us hints, but the reality is that it is going to blow us away. It will be beautiful. But the most important part of it is that we will be with God. We will experience Him. We will see Him face to face. We will see our Savior, Jesus, and speak with Him as a friend. We will see our loved ones who have died in the Lord. We will live our lives without the fear of death. There will be no more sadness. Everything will be in a state of "Shalom," of perfect peace and joy.

Dear reader, the Bible teaches us that after our lives on this earth, we will experience the joys of heaven. And that should give us great joy in the here and now. What can man do to us? As the apostle Paul discusses in Philippians 1:21-25, we are going to be better off by far to depart this life and be with Christ, but we all feel like we have some work to do still. Paul dealt with this tension. He makes the point at the end of this reading that our faith—even in the here and now—should give us joy. But the greatest joy, by far, will be for us to enter into God's rest, and have face-to-face fellowship with Jesus. Read this wonderful passage:

> For to me, to live is Christ and to die is gain. If I am to go on living in the body, this will mean fruitful labor for me. Yet what shall I choose? I do not know! I am torn between the two: I desire to depart and be with Christ, which is better by far, but it is more necessary for you that I remain in the body. Convinced of this, I know that I will remain, and I will continue with all of you for your progress and joy in the faith.

In other words, Paul says that while he loves this life, and it brings him great joy, he is quite ready to move on to be with Jesus. It's a wonderful glimpse into Paul's mind, and into his strong faith in the reality of Heaven.

Famously, Paul tells us that if we are home in our bodies, we are away from the Lord. But if we leave our bodies, we will be home with the Lord. Listen to what he says in 2 Corinthians 5:6-10:

> Therefore, we are always confident and know that as long as we are at home in the body we are away from the Lord. For we live by faith, not by sight. We are confident, I say, and would prefer to be away from the body and at home with the Lord. So we make it our goal to please him, whether we are at home in the body or away from it. For we must all appear before the judgment seat of Christ, so that each of us may receive what is due us for the things done while in the body, whether good or bad.

Heaven should make us leap for joy. Our Master, Jesus, tells us this. Listen to what He says in Luke 6:23a,

> "Rejoice in that day and leap for joy, because
> great is your reward in heaven."

I love how Jesus comforted his apostles when they were troubled and afraid. He gave them a brief description of heaven and told them he would prepare a place for them. We can take great joy in this promise from the Lord. He said this in John 14:1-4:

Do not let your hearts be troubled. You believe in God; believe also in me. My Father's house has many rooms; if that were not so, would I have told you that I am going there to prepare a place for you? And if I go and prepare a place for you, I will come back and take you to be with me that you also may be where I am. You know the way to the place where I am going.

Perhaps the most explicit descriptions of Heaven occur in the book of Revelation. The name of the book means "revealing." So, here is what is revealed about heaven in that book. We can first look at Revelation 21:1-7:

> Then I saw "a new heaven and a new earth,"
> for the first heaven and the first earth had
> passed away, and there was no longer any sea. I
> saw the Holy City, the new Jerusalem, coming
> down out of heaven from God, prepared as a
> bride beautifully dressed for her husband. And I
> heard a loud voice from the throne saying,
> "Look! God's dwelling place is now among the

people, and he will dwell with them. They will
be his people, and God himself will be with
them and be their God. 'He will wipe every tear
from their eyes. There will be no more death'
or mourning or crying or pain, for the old order
of things has passed away."

He who was seated on the throne said, "I am
making everything new!" Then he said, "Write
this down, for these words are trustworthy and
true."

He said to me: "It is done. I am the Alpha and
the Omega, the Beginning and the End. To the
thirsty I will give water without cost from the
spring of the water of life. Those who are victorious will inherit all this, and I will be their
God and they will be my children."

Later in that same chapter—Revelation 21—we read these wonderful and encouraging words (Revelation 21:19-27):

The foundations of the city walls were decorated with every kind of precious stone. The first
foundation was jasper, the second sapphire, the
third agate, the fourth emerald, the fifth onyx,
the sixth ruby, the seventh chrysolite, the eighth
beryl, the ninth topaz, the tenth turquoise, the
eleventh jacinth, and the twelfth amethyst. The
twelve gates were twelve pearls, each gate

made of a single pearl. The great street of the city was of gold, as pure as transparent glass.

I did not see a temple in the city, because the Lord God Almighty and the Lamb are its temple. The city does not need the sun or the moon to shine on it, for the glory of God gives it light, and the Lamb is its lamp. The nations will walk by its light, and the kings of the earth will bring their splendor into it. On no day will its gates ever be shut, for there will be no night there. The glory and honor of the nations will be brought into it. Nothing impure will ever enter it, nor will anyone who does what is shameful or deceitful, but only those whose names are written in the Lamb's book of life.

Then we get that wonderful passage where it says we will see the Lord face to face. It's found in Revelation 22:1-5:

Then the angel showed me the river of the water of life, as clear as crystal, flowing from the throne of God and of the Lamb down the middle of the great street of the city. On each side of the river stood the tree of life, bearing twelve crops of fruit, yielding its fruit every month. And the leaves of the tree are for the healing of the nations. No longer will there be any curse. The throne of God and of the Lamb will be in the city, and his servants will serve him. They will see his face, and his name will be on their foreheads. There will be no more night. They

will not need the light of a lamp or the light of
the sun, for the Lord God will give them light.
And they will reign for ever and ever.

I want to conclude this chapter by letting you know that the reality of heaven should bring you joy. Heaven awaits your loved ones who die in Christ. You have that to look forward to.

You may have lost your parents. I realize you may have lost close friends, as I have. Some of you have lost a spouse, and some of you have lost a child. This is all so painful to think about and to talk about. But what should give you deep joy is that you will see them again. You will dance with them. You will worship Jesus with them, with broad smiles and glad hearts. All of that is coming. And you can look forward to that with so much anticipation and joy.

Heaven is going to be wonderful. We will see our Lord Jesus Christ face to face. All worry and stress will be gone. We will have no more sorrows. Our eternity will be full of adventure and peace as we explore all that God has for us to do. I promise you we won't be playing harps and sitting on clouds. That's ridiculous. But what we will experience is joy, and all of the joyful activities our Father has planned for us. We will worship Him, and serve Him, with great gladness in our hearts.

I can only imagine. It is going to be so beautiful. We can only imagine.

Homework

For homework, I hope you will find some time to recline and to imagine heaven, and to imagine seeing your loved ones who have died in Christ. And smile. Let it fill you with unspeakable joy.

12. Have an Attitude of Gratitude

In the last chapter of this book, titled "Joy in the Morning," our lesson has to do with "Having an Attitude of Gratitude." As you'll recall, the key idea of this book has been that if you start your day with God, then you are likely to experience His joy all throughout the day.

My goal for this chapter is that each of us will depart from here with a greater commitment to counting our blessings, being grateful, and thanking God for what we have, rather than being pessimistic about the things that we don't have.

I think we all know that joy is closely linked with gratitude. If we are constantly thinking about the things that are not right in our lives, or if we focus on our negative experiences, or if we spend our time counting our losses, then we are not going to be joyful.

In fact, those ways of thinking accomplish just the opposite. If you spend your life lamenting the things you lost, then you lose sight of the things you found. You had a falling out with a friend when you were in college? Well, that may have happened, but look at what you gained! You made many, many friends in college, and you are still connected to some of them. Or perhaps you had a bad day on Thursday. Well, what about the good day you're having today? Maybe you're thinking about the money you lost back in 2009 with the housing crisis. Well, what about all of the years since, as clearly God has provided for you to get you to where you are today?

It can be toxic to focus on what you don't have, rather than focusing on what you've been blessed with. Think about your friends. Do you have any friends that want to sit around and talk about the negative? I can tell you that they are very likely thinking about what they don't have. They are focusing on the wrong things. They're thinking about how they don't get paid enough, or they don't like many things about America, or they're complaining about this or that in their job.

Well, let's look at the opposite. Instead of focusing on your money not being enough, why don't you focus on the fact that you have been blessed with plenty of money to survive! It all depends upon who you're comparing yourself to. If I compare myself to Elon Musk, then —boy—I'm pretty destitute. But if I remind myself that I live in the United States, and I have been given an education, and I have a place to call home here in California... if I have all of those things, I'm pretty much in the world's top 5%!

Similarly, you have a choice. You can complain about America, or you can thank God for America, and be proud to be an American. You can complain about our Social Security system, or you can thank God that you have a check coming in each month once you hit 65. You can complain about your job, or you can thank God for your job. Seeing that you're in the United States of America, you can also get another good job. You don't have to live your life in misery. This country provides more opportunity than any other nation in the world. That's why the U.S. has always been known as the "Land of Opportunity." You can work hard and become something in this land. You can complain about your spouse, or you can give thanks for your spouse. You can complain about your children, or you can give thanks for your children. You can complain your life away, or you can thank God each and every day. It's all up to you!

One of my favorite scriptures in the Bible comes from 1 Thessalonians 5:16-18. Read this very concise passage. It really gets to the point:

> Rejoice always, pray continually, give thanks in
> all circumstances; for this is God's will for you
> in Christ Jesus.

The apostle Paul connects rejoicing with prayer, and with giving thanks in "all circumstances." This is God's will for us.

Each one of us has a choice to make, and it is a far better choice to thank God as opposed to complaining about things. Instead of "complaining" in all circumstances, we should change our minds and "give thanks" in all circumstances. We should have an attitude of gratitude. Be grateful for what you have.

When we focus on what's wrong, we start to convince ourselves that everything in our lives is wrong. That things are out of sorts. We'll start convincing ourselves that life is bad, and we should have an axe to grind. The Bible says, "No." The grateful person thinks about the good. She thinks about what God has given to her. She rejoices that God has given her life. The positive person counts up how many blessings she's had today, rather than counting up all the things she didn't get this week.

For some of us, we were trained to think about the negative. Perhaps it was modeled for us by someone who thought negatively all the time, so we have a hard time with this lesson. I've heard it said that our minds naturally drift to the negative because of our ancient roots, living in the wild and trying to survive. The theory is that we evolved to think about problems and threats. "Is a bear going to come into our cave? Is a snake hidden somewhere in the grass? Is an earthquake going to come? Are we going to have enough food and clothing for the winter?"

They say that our minds are naturally hard-wired to think like this. We had to think about potential dangers and threats in order to avoid them when they did come. And so, the theory goes, we have evolved to live in fear. We've evolved to catastrophize. We've learned to focus on our lack rather than focus on our blessings.

Well, that may be so. Granted, maybe the cave men and women did need to think about the saber-tooth tiger. But you know what? The saber-tooth tiger went extinct, and we didn't!

Today, we don't have to live in fear. We can live our lives with thankfulness in our hearts. We can live with gladness and joy. We don't have to fear. Even if there are things in our lives that are scary, we don't have to focus on them. Focusing on the things that scare you will absolutely ruin your life!

I knew a woman who was mistreated by her father when she was a girl. He was a mean man, angry, and negative. He was intimidating. This girl grew up to be a woman who literally hurt all the people around her because they were a threat to her. She became a suspicious person, full of fear. Worst of all, she became a female version of her father: intimidating, always angry, and always hurting people because she was living with hurt in her heart. She had no true friends, and the friends she did have would come and go with the seasons.

Another passage in the Bible that links joy with gratitude is in Philippians 4:4-7. Listen to what Paul says,

> Rejoice in the Lord always. I will say it again: Rejoice! Let your gentleness be evident to all. The Lord is near. Do not be anxious about anything, but in every situation, by prayer and petition, with thanksgiving, present your requests to God. And the peace of God, which transcends all understanding, will guard your hearts and your minds in Christ Jesus.

Once again, Paul connects rejoicing (or, joy) with prayer, and also with thanksgiving—or "gratitude." Have an attitude of gratitude.

You know, sometimes I think Paul may have struggled with anxiety or depression. You know what else I think? I think he overcame those things. I think that while he may have struggled with such conditions in his youth, as he matured, he learned how to outsmart his pessimistic outlook. And he did it through prayer and good thinking. In the very next passage, Paul gives the kind of advice that you might hear from a therapist today! Listen to what he says about what you should do with your thinking. This occurs in Philippians 4:8:

> Finally, brothers and sisters, whatever is true, whatever is noble, whatever is right, whatever is pure, whatever is lovely, whatever is admirable—if anything is excellent or praiseworthy—think about such things.

We have included this passage several times throughout the book thus far, but it is good advice, worth repeating and internalizing. Here we have Paul explicitly saying that we should think about good things, and not let our minds spiral down the black rabbit hole where everything is negative, everyone is a threat, and nobody is good. That's actually a kind of mental hell. If your mind ever starts to go to that mental hell, then I want to encourage you to revisit Philippians 4. Rejoice and give thanks. Present your requests to God. Enjoy God's peace that comes after good, hard prayer. Think about good things. Think about admirable things. Think about things that are excellent.

Recently, I was having a good talk with some folks from church, and we were talking about similar topics brought up in this chapter. One of them brought up a song by Amy Grant. The song is called "Find What You're Looking For," and it describes all of us. We all have secrets, darkness, and shameful histories, but we also have kindness, goodness, sacrifice, and love in our hearts. Check out these powerful lyrics when you have the chance.

And that pretty much summarizes the point I've been trying to make. We'll often just find what we're looking for. We get to choose. And we often choose to view people with suspicion and pessimism. God does give you the freedom to view them as flawed people—but you also have the freedom to see people's capability for good. Just like you and me. We're both flawed, but we're also full of compassion and love.

If you choose to view someone with suspicion, or if you choose to view them as bad, then try hard to change your thinking. Try to view them the way God views them. People, with problems, but with potential.

Dear reader, I'd like to end this book with a wonderful verse from Colossians 2:6-7. It is the perfect verse to close this written quest for joy.

> So then, just as you received Christ Jesus as Lord, continue to live your lives in him, rooted and built up in him, strengthened in the faith as you were taught, and overflowing with thankfulness.

The great apostle Paul tells us here to continue on living life in Jesus. Get rooted in Jesus. Build your faith in Jesus. Become strong in your faith. Exercise those faith muscles. And do it all with great thankfulness. In fact,

Paul says to do it while you "overflow with thankfulness."

That's excellent advice for us as we try to live with an attitude of gratitude.

And it is also one of the great secrets to having a life of joy. Instead of simply being grateful, "overflow with thankfulness." Count your blessings often. Thank people for what they've done for you. Text people words of thankfulness. Pray to God, and thank Him for all He's done in your life. Thank your spouse for doing the dishes, or bringing you a cup of coffee.

As I was preparing this chapter, I ruminated on the expression "Overflowing with thankfulness." What exactly does that mean?

I think it means this—have you ever walked with a glass full of some liquid in your hand? Maybe a full cup of coffee from Starbucks. Now, imagine someone bumping into you, and some of the coffee spills out. If we are full of bitterness and negativity, then guess what comes out whenever we get bumped—that's right. Our bitterness. But if you are "overflowing with gratefulness," then you will spill joy and thanksgiving whenever someone bumps into you.

You cannot hide what you are full of. Jesus says this in Luke 6:43-45:

> No good tree bears bad fruit, nor does a bad tree bear good fruit. Each tree is recognized by its own fruit. People do not pick figs from thornbushes, or grapes from briers. A good man brings good things out of the good stored up in

his heart, and an evil man brings evil things out of the evil stored up in his heart. For the mouth speaks what the heart is full of.

If your heart is full of fear, guess what's going to come out? You're going to speak words of fear, worry, anxiety, and concern. You'll spend your time spinning your brain in circles, wondering how to prevent bad things from happening. You'll worry yourself to death. You'll die a thousand deaths and suffer a thousand humiliations. All because your heart is full of fear.

Similarly, if you have anger inside of you, you'll focus on how to get vengeance on the person who wronged you. You'll get bitter when people say something negative about you. You'll lose your temper and your self-control. You'll bark at people. You'll even strike out at people. Anger can destroy you.

We have got to work on these bad habits, like worry, anxiety, anger, and bitterness. We have got to be people who spill joy. We need to become people who "overflow with thanksgiving."

Jesus says that we speak out of the overflow of our hearts. If we are full of good thoughts and good intentions, we will spill out joy and gratitude.

Dear reader… this book on joy is over. If there are only three ideas from this volume that I can leave you with, it is this:

- Try to always have an attitude of gratitude.

- If your mind starts going down the black rabbit hole of negativity, then do as Paul says and change your thinking. Think about good things.

- And, finally, I think a crucial lesson in this book is: if you really want joy… if you really want to be a person who has joy in their heart, who speaks words of joy, and who walks with a bounce in your step… stay connected to the vine.

Jesus says, "I am the vine … you are the branches." If each one of us stays connected to Him, then we'll be fine. We'll be more than fine. We'll be full of joy.

Stay connected to the vine and YOU'LL be full of joy.

That's your homework. To be a person of joy—stay connected to Jesus.

About the Author

If you feel generous and have a few minutes, please leave a review online where you purchased this book. It makes a significant difference to the author. Thank you in advance.

Dyron B. Daughrity is the William S. Banowsky Chair in Religion at Pepperdine University in Malibu, California. He is the author of many books and articles in the fields of comparative religion, global Christianity, and world religious history. He has ministered to churches for over 30 years, and is currently the Senior Minister at the Hilltop Community Church of Christ in El Segundo, California. Dyron has been married to Sunde for 28 years and they have four children.

Visit the author's website at:
https://seaver.pepperdine.edu/academics/faculty/dyron-daughrity/

Follow on social media
https://www.facebook.com/dyron.daughrity

About the Publisher

Sulis International Press publishes select fiction and nonfiction in a variety of genres under four imprints:

- Riversong Books (fiction)
- Sulis Press (general nonfiction)
- Keledei Publications (spirituality)
- Sulis Academic Press (academic works)

For more, visit the website at
https://sulisinternational.com

Subscribe to the newsletter at
https://sulisinternational.com/subscribe/

Follow on social media
https://www.facebook.com/SulisInternational
https://twitter.com/Sulis_Intl
https://www.pinterest.com/Sulis_Intl/
https://www.instagram.com/sulis_international/

www.ingramcontent.com/pod-product-compliance
Lightning Source LLC
Chambersburg PA
CBHW032126090426
42743CB00007B/479